50 STRATEGIES FOR INTEGRATING AI INTO THE CLASSROOM

Donnie Piercey, M.Ed.

To Raven,
for listening to years of my
educational musings.

Publishing Credits

Corinne Burton, M.A.Ed., *President* and *Publisher*
Aubrie Nielsen, M.S.Ed., *EVP of Content Development*
Kyra Ostendorf, M.Ed., *Publisher, professional books*
James Anderson, M.S.Ed., *VP of Digital Product*
Véronique Bos, *Vice President of Creative*
Tom Rademacher, M.Ed., *Developmental Editor*
Christine Zuchora-Walske, *Senior Editorial Manager*
Andrew Greene, M.A.Ed., *Senior Content Manager*
Avery Rabedeaux, *Assistant Editor*
Kevin Pham, *Graphic Designer*

Image Credits

Images page 11, 82, and 94 Donnie Piercey with Midjourney; all other images iStock and/or Shutterstock

Shell Education

A division of Teacher Created Materials
5482 Argosy Avenue
Huntington Beach, CA 92649
www.tcmpub.com/shell-education
ISBN 979-8-7659-4710-4
© 2024 Shell Educational Publishing, Inc.

Printed by: 995
Printed in: U.S.A.
PO#: PO13599

Table of Contents

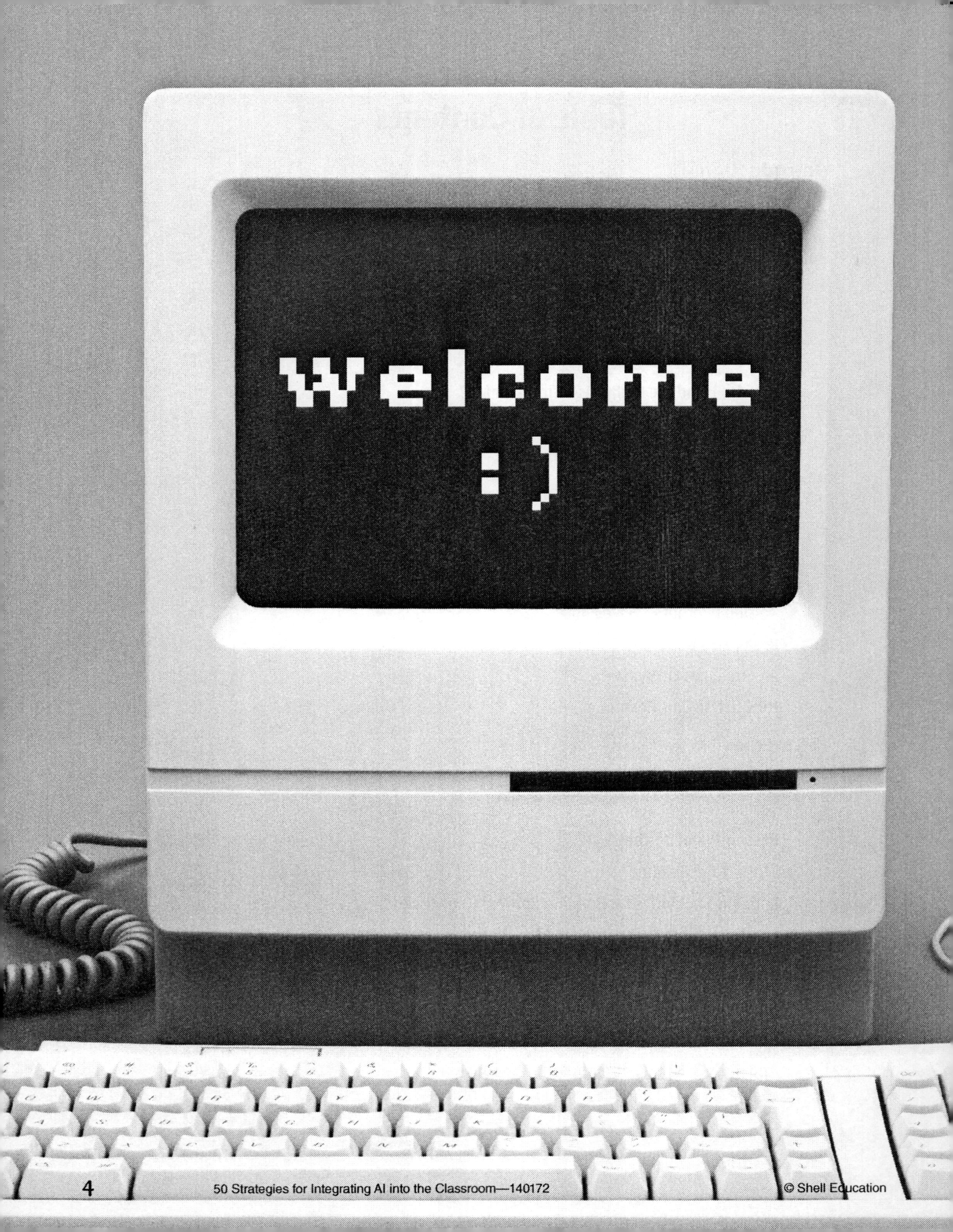
Welcome
:)

I've been a classroom teacher in Kentucky since 2007. The technology in my first classroom included a whiteboard and an overhead projector that I struggled to use every day. A decade and a half later, technology has changed so much that I now must include this assurance in the opening paragraph of my book: Artificial intelligence (AI) did not write this. It was written by a human: me, Donnie Piercey. I promise.

If you're brand-new to AI tools, no worries! I've designed the strategies in this book for both experts and beginners to read, play with, tweak, and teach.

As you explore the various AI tools and ideas presented in this book, please remember that every class and student is unique. And as incredible as artificial intelligence has become, it hasn't changed these three essential truths about teaching:

Good pedagogy is <u>still important.</u>

Developing positive relationships with students <u>still matters.</u>

Read-alouds (with paper books!) are <u>still cool.</u>

Meeting the Newest New Thing in Education

I've found that most educators have some variation of this experience when they see AI in action for the first time:

1. Teacher copies and pastes essay question to see what AI creates.

2. AI answers said essay question.

3. Teacher deems it a B- essay at best.

4. Teacher asks AI to turn the essay response into a sea shanty sung in a minor key with the accompanying chords.

5. AI does it in seconds.

6. Teacher spits out coffee.

When I started experimenting with AI, I had an experience similar to the first time I used Google Search or YouTube. I thought, "Wait, what *else* can this thing do? I need to figure this out, because things are going to change in the classroom, and in a hurry." And I believe there's a strong chance that fifty years from now a teacher will pick up this book and chuckle at some of the ways we *thought* AI was going to affect the classroom.

If you're thinking that artificial intelligence is some scary future thing, you can take a deep breath and relax. There's no need to dread its arrival. It's already here, and it's only going to get better. For the students walking through the doors of your classroom today, the AI they'll encounter is the most nonhumanlike AI they'll ever experience (de la Higuera 2019).

If you remember America Online (AOL) or Netscape Navigator from the 1990s, the champions of the early internet, you know what I mean. Apps like ChatGPT are groundbreaking, but they're the Netscape Navigator of AI. We're just getting started (Dwivedi et al. 2023). AI apps are evolving faster than a middle schooler's mood, so expect new and improved tools to keep popping up as classroom teachers figure out creative ways to use these tools with their students.

I realize this may be a little terrifying. Let's address the robot in the room. You know, the whole "Bots are going to take over the world" worry. Sure, we might joke about our future robot overlords, but the truth is: AI offers more ways to help than to hinder classroom instruction (Gillani 2023). You can rest easy knowing that your job is safe from the clutches of a fleet of TeacherBots. For now.

Now let's talk about the elephant in the room (it's a big room—full of robots and elephants): student academic integrity. You might think that introducing AI to a classroom is just asking for trouble, like handing over the answers to a test. But I believe that a student's first instinct *isn't* to cheat. Kids are naturally curious, and

AI can be a powerful tool to ignite their spark of curiosity and guide them toward meaningful learning experiences.

My goal in this book is to show you how to use AI responsibly, keeping the focus on learning, student creativity, and engagement. I'm hoping it will make your teaching life easier—that you'll be able to pick it up and dive into some classroom activities with your students today (especially if you happen to be reading this during your 45-minute planning block or 22.5-minute lunch).

The book covers all sorts of AI, from virtual tutors and grading assistants to personalized learning plans and interactive simulations. It does not focus on specific apps. You can use whatever apps you like, including the ones no one knows about yet.

The practical tips and real-world examples in this book can help you get the most out of using AI in your classroom. Whether you're a tech-savvy educator or a newbie to the digital realm, I've got you covered.

So, grab your coffee (which will one day be brewed by a robot butler) and get ready to ride into the wild world of AI. Remember: the future is bright, the bots are (mostly) friendly, and we're all in this together.

Questions to Consider Before Using AI in the Classroom

As AI continues to advance, it will offer numerous opportunities to make the classroom and learning experience more engaging, efficient, and personalized. To harness the full potential of AI in the classroom, you'll need to plan for and use AI-powered tools and resources that cater to your students' diverse needs. Here are some important questions to consider as you bring AI into your classroom:

- What are the learning targets, goals, or objectives for this lesson, and how can AI tools help me achieve them?
- What prior knowledge do my students have, and how can AI help me identify and fill any learning gaps?
- How can AI save me time on tedious tasks so I can spend more time helping my students succeed?
- How can I use AI tools to offer personalized feedback and guidance for each student?
- When should students be guided by AI during practice exercises to ensure understanding?
- How can AI-powered apps assist me in teaching and reinforcing new content-specific vocabulary?
- In what ways can I use AI to help formatively assess student learning?
- How can AI tools help me model complex concepts and processes for students?
- How can AI help me monitor student progress and determine when learning objectives are met?
- What AI-driven interventions or resources can I provide for students who need additional support?
- How can I use AI for collaborative learning and peer-to-peer interactions?

The answers to the above questions may change depending on the day and the activity. Some of these questions may never have perfect answers for you, but asking them will help you focus your intentions and lesson planning on what you know is most important.

What Role Does Creativity Play?

AI tools can provide a personalized learning experience tailored to individual students' needs, but it is ultimately up to the students to explore, experiment, and innovate with these resources. By encouraging creativity, you can empower your students to think critically and create unique solutions to problems, which can lead to a deeper understanding of content. This creative mindset will serve them well as they move from school to adulthood, where AI will continue to play a role in many fields.

Yeah, but Can't They Just Use This to Cheat?

As AI technologies become more pervasive in schools, the need to have discussions with students about what role AI *should* play is growing. You'll want to teach students the importance of honesty, accountability, and respect in using AI tools. Students must understand the consequences of actions such as using an app like ChatGPT or Bard to do their homework for them. There's still value in the students' productive struggle.

AI Is a Tool for Learning, Not a Replacement for It

As a teacher, it's your responsibility to learn how to use AI so you can pass on this knowledge to your students. By familiarizing yourself with AI technologies, you can use them to create meaningful, engaging, and interactive learning experiences. Additionally, you must serve as a role model by demonstrating the ethical use of AI and promoting the values of creativity and integrity in how *you* use it.

In an AI-driven world, it is crucial to give students opportunities for hands-on experience and guidance. This includes incorporating AI-powered applications in lessons, encouraging collaboration on AI-related projects, and having deep discussions on the ethical implications of AI. By exposing students to the real-world uses of AI and allowing them to experiment with these tools, you can help them develop the skills and mindset they need to succeed in whatever robot-overlord-driven world they end up graduating into.

Though AI is an important tool, I don't think this means that kindergarteners need to be introduced to it on the first day of school. As much as I love technology, there's still so much value in having students read a good book and do other unplugged learning. No matter when or how much you use AI in our classrooms, you need to do so thoughtfully. Researchers at MIT are finding that the most productive AI education uses are rooted in three design principles: Active Learning, Embedded Ethics, and Low Barriers to Access (Williams et al. 2022).

How Do I Find the Right AI Platform for Me?

As you flip through this book, you'll read about various AI apps. Most are free, but some require a subscription or one-time payment. New options are coming out all the time, so search for the app that best fits your educational needs and budget. ChatGPT and Bard are examples of *generative* AI that can assist in composing, creating writing prompts, or even offering feedback on student work. But AI is more than just text. You can also use AI to create images, music, animations, and (probably sooner than we think) movies. Dall-E and Midjourney are two examples of image-generating AI tools.

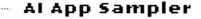

AI App Sampler

Document Creation (Chatbots)

- ChatGPT (chat.openai.com/chat): Need a hand with lesson planning or content creation? Let ChatGPT be your assistant! It has both free and paid plans. Paid plans offer higher speed.

- Bard (bard.google.com): Spark your students' creativity with Bard, Google's chatbot that'll create story ideas and refine writing.

- Magic Write (canva.com/magic-write): The Canva design platform includes a Magic Write option that'll create text, poems, and paragraphs in seconds. Both free and paid options are available.

- Help Me Write: Watch for this new AI writing assistant built into Google Docs and Gmail.

Image Creation

- Midjourney (midjourney.com): This app lets you create custom images in seconds. Midjourney starts free, but it turns into a paid service once you've created a certain number of images.

- Dall-E (openai.com/product/dall-e-2): This AI-powered image generator will create visuals based on your text descriptions. The first fifty images are free. After that, Dall-E becomes a paid service.

- Adobe Firefly (adobe.com/firefly): This assistant, currently a beta version, will eventually be built into Adobe's Creative Cloud. It's quite good at creating beautiful graphics.

- Shutterstock AI Image Generator (shutterstock.com/generate): Create custom visuals for your lessons with this image creator. Free and paid services are available.

- Canva AI Image Generator (canva.com/ai-image-generator): For those of you who use Canva, this tool is a great way to create images for projects you're designing.

Chatbots as Teaching Assistants and Learning Tools

Generative chatbots are changing the ways educators teach and interact with students. These AI-driven conversational tools can understand and respond to natural-language questions, providing instant support to both teachers and students.

You can use chatbots as teaching assistants. They can help you manage your workload by answering routine questions, offering personalized feedback, and assisting in lesson planning (Chinonso, Adalikwu, and Tolorunleke 2023). Try a simple prompt such as *I am trying to come up with a creative way to teach my students how to [insert skill here]*. You'll be surprised at what the chatbot comes up with.

AI chatbots can also serve as engaging learning tools for students. They can offer explanations, examples, and clarifications on a wide range of topics in real time, catering to the individual needs of each student. Students have reported positive results using ChatGPT as a "personal tutor" that "patiently" answers questions (Tlili et al. 2023). If a student is struggling to understand a concept, they can ask AI follow-up questions until the puzzle pieces start coming together. This is personalized learning. Instead of telling a student to watch a YouTube video over and over until they finally get how to balance an equation, now students can read (or maybe watch) a response to a question, and then ask a chatbot clarifying questions to hone their understanding.

Even better, chatbots extend beyond classroom management and support. You can use these advanced AI systems to encourage critical thinking and creative problem-solving among your students. By posing open-ended questions or providing prompts, you can use AI to stimulate discussions and debates on various subjects. Chatbots can offer counterarguments, alternative perspectives, or additional information, helping students develop a more comprehensive understanding of the material being discussed or taught in class (Chinonso, Adalikwu, and Tolorunleke 2023).

Another advantage of using chatbots in a classroom is their ability to adapt to the learning needs of individual students. By analyzing student interactions, a chatbot can identify areas where a learner might need extra help, tailor a response to address those needs, and provide personalized feedback for further study (Kasneci et al. 2023).

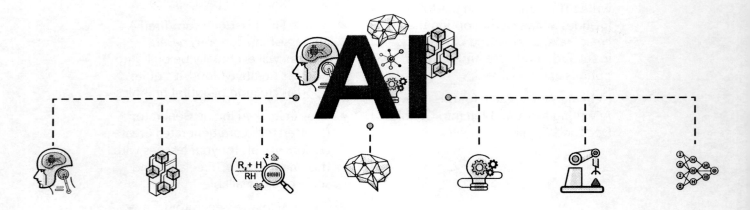

Wait . . . AI Does Pictures Too?

AI can create images in seconds. The advanced algorithms behind these tools can create unique and diverse images based on whatever prompts a student enters. Image generators are a powerful way for students to explore a relationship between language and the visual arts. You will want to be careful depending on the age of your students. Although most AI generators won't create overtly inappropriate images, they can sometimes create images that are unsettling or scary.

AI image generators are also just delightful to play with. For example, let's imagine that I wanted a creative writing prompt for my students. I asked Midjourney to create an image of *a girl looking inside a strange box she discovered inside a tree*. Midjourney made the following image in seconds.

Image created by Donnie Piercey with Midjourney. Reprinted with permission.

Looks like a great story starter to me!

Using AI Effectively

Learning to use AI effectively will help you create a more engaging and constructive learning experience for your students. There's a huge difference between the prompt *Write about video games* and the prompt *Write five paragraphs at a high school reading level about the video game console wars and the economic impact on consumers.* Just as with a web search engine, you'll need to learn the most effective ways to use AI tools to get the best results.

Tweak It

Although artificial intelligence has made significant strides in recent years and will continue to do so, it is important to remember that these tools are far from perfect. The algorithms behind AI tools are not always able to grasp the nuances and context of what you want it to create. Sometimes, the prompt you give ChatGPT just doesn't give you the response you're looking for.

As with everything else you do for your students, you must be prepared to adjust and refine your use of AI to serve your students effectively. This is crucial to ensuring that the AI-generated content caters to the specific needs, interests, and learning preferences of our students.

It is common for AI-generated content to miss the mark. So tweak it! Be prepared to double-check everything and adjust as needed. This process may involve refining the input prompt, providing some context, or even breaking down complex ideas into simpler components. The more practice you get working with AI, the more practice it gets working with you. For example, when I got my first smart speaker in my home, it worked better and better the more I learned how to talk to it.

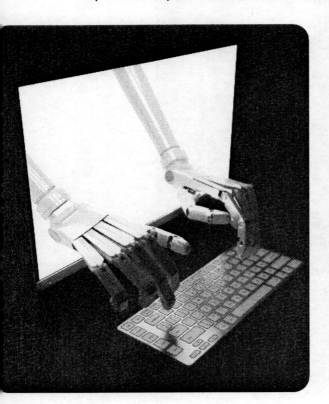

How Will You Know If Students Cheat?

Let me be clear: I don't believe that a student's first instinct is to cheat. But sometimes temptation gets the better of the best of us. That's why it's important for you to have a few tricks up your sleeve for when stress, time, or temptation gets the best of your students. Many AI detection apps can help you determine when something's just a little too . . . well . . . robotic.

Show your students that these tools exist and that you know how to use them. This can help you maintain academic integrity in your classroom by preventing AI shenanigans. And when you know how to use AI detectors, you can keep a keen eye on students' work to make sure they're actually learning and not just relying on their robot friends.

But AI detectors aren't all rainbows and unicorns. Sometimes they might give you false positives or negatives. So, while they can be helpful, it's important not to rely on them entirely. Also, be cautious about the potential impact on student trust. You don't want to create an atmosphere where your students feel like they're constantly under suspicion. Using AI detectors should be just one part of your overall approach to promoting academic integrity.

AI Ethics

The transformation that AI has brought to us already is incredible. Heck, yesterday my wife ordered a coffee that was delivered to her office by a four-wheeled robot. But it's important to talk about some of the ethical dilemmas that come with such advancements. Not everyone is overjoyed at the emergence of AI, which is a tool that combines more than it creates. Visual artists—especially digital artists—have protested that their original work is visible and recognizable in AI images without their permission. Many people have concerns about what AI means for the future of art, writing, and other pursuits long considered distinctly human. Big questions are arising—questions you are likely bringing up with your students—and we don't have answers for them yet.

- How can AI inspire students without replacing human creativity?
- How can original artists be acknowledged?
- When is it okay to use AI, and when is it not?
- How much can you trust what AI tells you?
- How can you tell if AI is missing an important perspective?

By having open dialogues with your students and colleagues about these questions, you can guide your students into a future where tech turns into an ally rather than an occupying force. And of course, always check AI-generated content to ensure it's what you want it to be. As with all teaching materials, you will need to review and make choices about AI and help students learn about using it constructively.

One recent article by David Baidoo-Anu and co-authors listed the possible drawbacks of using ChatGPT or similar AI in education as lack of human interaction, limited understanding, bias in training data, lack of creativity, and privacy (Baidoo-Anu and Owusu Ansah 2023). The author credited with that section of the article was, it turns out, ChatGPT. So, it's complex.

As AI-generated narratives and art become more common, focus on celebrating the creativity, connections, and discoveries your students make, not just the speed of work completion. I hope the rise of AI will mean that human creators, storytellers, musicians, writers, poets, and artists are celebrated at a much deeper level. It's the human touch, encouraging our students to pursue knowledge, that truly makes a difference in every classroom.

Don't Forget to Have Fun!

Go ahead: dip your toes into the AI pool and see how it feels. Visit an image-generating website and see what you can create. Go and ask a chatbot to rewrite the ending to your favorite movie. Don't like what it creates? Ask it to try again.

Our time is stretched thin enough as it is; grading papers, planning lessons, and managing a classroom are no small feats. So why not explore ways that technology can enhance and streamline your experience? By embracing AI, you could save time and energy, giving you more opportunities to work one-on-one with your students and have a real impact on their lives (Chinonso, Adalikwu, and Tolorunleke 2023).

Break This Book

This book contains fifty strategies, and it can open the door to an infinite world of new ideas, new possibilities, new tools, and new ways to teach and learn. The great—and sometimes overwhelming—thing about artificial intelligence is that no one knows everything it can do now, much less in a year or five years.

The strategies here are meant to empower you to experiment and find the best ways to enhance student learning in your classroom, all while encouraging curiosity and creativity. I'm a firm believer that the best way to learn about new things is to play with them until they break, then see how the insides work.

In each strategy in this book, you'll see a sample prompt. The sample prompts are by no means the only prompts that will work (or the prompts that will work best with whatever version of AI you're using). They're a starting point for you to build on. Appendix B contains a list of all these prompts and sample responses that AI created from them.

While you try these strategies, listen for your inner voice asking, "What if . . . ?" or, "I wonder . . . " and try those things. Try ridiculous things. Try things that make you laugh. Try things you're absolutely sure won't work. And remember, AI is a tool that talks back. So if you get lost, ask it where to go next, ask it how to fix the thing that's not working, ask it for another idea or five or fifty. You are among the first group of teachers who will become experts in teaching with AI. You're an explorer, and it's a fun tool to get lost with.

Strategies Overview

The strategies in this book are organized into the following sections to help you find the ideas you need most.

Teacher Time-Savers

In this chapter, I share some AI tools that will help you work more efficiently, spend more time with students, and use more of your time and energy doing what you love: teaching. I hope these clever workflows will help you find the balance you need.

Lesson-Planning Tools

There will be times when you hit a creative wall, and that's when AI can come to your rescue! These digital companions can bring fresh ideas to your classroom by suggesting innovative and engaging activities tailored to your students' needs. AI can jump-start your teaching brain, making sure you're never scrambling to figure out how you're going to teach the content.

Writing and Reading

Because AI communicates mostly through text (for now), the options available for inventive, engaging, differentiated writing and reading strategies get their own chapter. When ChatGPT launched, writing and reading teachers had some questions and concerns about what it could do. In this chapter you'll learn how to create stories tailored for each student's interests and the skill practice they need, how to develop Choose Your Own Adventure–style writing and reading activities, and more.

Engaging Activities for Building Content Knowledge

This chapter highlights flexible strategies to help students build content knowledge across disciplines and inspire engagement and inquiry. AI can help you build, adapt, or assist lessons by creating unique data, connecting ideas and themes across content, and giving students new ways to show their learning.

Fun Time! (or How I Learned to Stop Worrying and Love Indoor Recess)

We've all had those days. We've all had *so many* of those days. Something gets canceled or announced at the last minute, you're voluntold to sub without a plan, you and your students return from a field trip with an hour left in the day, or you age decades during a single indoor recess. This chapter is full of games and activities you can pull together quickly to fill those times, build some community, and have some fun.

How to Use This Resource

On each strategy page, you'll find an idea accompanied by prompt suggestions that you can enter into whatever AI app you're using. You can use the prompts exactly as they are or modify them to suit your students' unique needs. Almost all the strategies in this book can be expanded or adapted to fit many grade levels and topics.

Sample prompts give you examples of what to type into AI to get started.

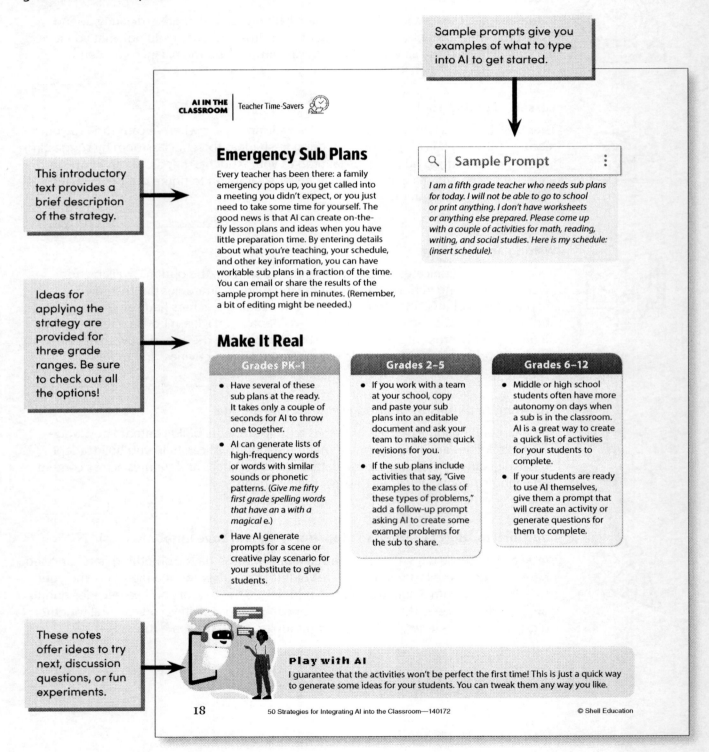

AI IN THE CLASSROOM | Teacher Time-Savers

Emergency Sub Plans

This introductory text provides a brief description of the strategy.

Every teacher has been there: a family emergency pops up, you get called into a meeting you didn't expect, or you just need to take some time for yourself. The good news is that AI can create on-the-fly lesson plans and ideas when you have little preparation time. By entering details about what you're teaching, your schedule, and other key information, you can have workable sub plans in a fraction of the time. You can email or share the results of the sample prompt here in minutes. (Remember, a bit of editing might be needed.)

🔍 | Sample Prompt ⋮

I am a fifth grade teacher who needs sub plans for today. I will not be able to go to school or print anything. I don't have worksheets or anything else prepared. Please come up with a couple of activities for math, reading, writing, and social studies. Here is my schedule: (insert schedule).

Make It Real

Ideas for applying the strategy are provided for three grade ranges. Be sure to check out all the options!

Grades PK–1

- Have several of these sub plans at the ready. It takes only a couple of seconds for AI to throw one together.
- AI can generate lists of high-frequency words or words with similar sounds or phonetic patterns. (*Give me fifty first grade spelling words that have an a with a magical e.*)
- Have AI generate prompts for a scene or creative play scenario for your substitute to give students.

Grades 2–5

- If you work with a team at your school, copy and paste your sub plans into an editable document and ask your team to make some quick revisions for you.
- If the sub plans include activities that say, "Give examples to the class of these types of problems," add a follow-up prompt asking AI to create some example problems for the sub to share.

Grades 6–12

- Middle or high school students often have more autonomy on days when a sub is in the classroom. AI is a great way to create a quick list of activities for your students to complete.
- If your students are ready to use AI themselves, give them a prompt that will create an activity or generate questions for them to complete.

These notes offer ideas to try next, discussion questions, or fun experiments.

Play with AI

I guarantee that the activities won't be perfect the first time! This is just a quick way to generate some ideas for your students. You can tweak them any way you like.

18   50 Strategies for Integrating AI into the Classroom—140172   © Shell Education

Strategies Table of Contents

Teacher Time-Savers

Lesson-Planning Tools

Writing and Reading

Engaging Activities for Building Content Knowledge

Fun Time! (or How I Learned to Stop Worrying and Love Indoor Recess)

Emergency Sub Plans

Every teacher has been there: a family emergency pops up, you get called into a meeting you didn't expect, or you just need to take some time for yourself. The good news is that AI can create on-the-fly lesson plans and ideas when you have little preparation time. By entering details about what you're teaching, your schedule, and other key information, you can have workable sub plans in a fraction of the time. You can email or share the results of the sample prompt here in minutes. (Remember, a bit of editing might be needed.)

🔍 **Sample Prompt** ⋮

I am a fifth grade teacher who needs sub plans for today. I will not be able to go to school or print anything. I don't have worksheets or anything else prepared. Please come up with a couple of activities for math, reading, writing, and social studies. Here is my schedule: (insert schedule).

Make It Real

Grades PK–1

- Have several of these sub plans at the ready. It takes only a couple of seconds for AI to throw one together.
- AI can generate lists of high-frequency words or words with similar sounds or phonetic patterns. (*Give me fifty first grade spelling words that have an a with a magical e.*)
- Have AI generate prompts for a scene or creative play scenario for your substitute to give students.

Grades 2–5

- If you work with a team at your school, copy and paste your sub plans into an editable document and ask your team to make some quick revisions for you.
- If the sub plans include activities that say, "Give examples to the class of these types of problems," add a follow-up prompt asking AI to create some example problems for the sub to share.

Grades 6–12

- Middle or high school students often have more autonomy on days when a sub is in the classroom. AI is a great way to create a quick list of activities for your students to complete.
- If your students are ready to use AI themselves, give them a prompt that will create an activity or generate questions for them to complete.

Play with AI

I guarantee that the activities won't be perfect the first time! This is just a quick way to generate some ideas for your students. You can tweak them any way you like.

Study Schedule

As teachers, we spend a lot of time helping our students (and ourselves) stay organized. For those of us who don't delight in creating calendars and schedules, chatbots can do the heavy lifting—and maybe give us some new ideas along the way.

🔍 **Sample Prompt** ⋮

Create a one-week study schedule for fourth graders to help them learn the water cycle. Include specific vocabulary and activities that students can do at home for practice.

Make It Real

Grades PK–1

- Customize the week for little learners in seconds: ask AI to create a plan to teach your students specific phonemes or an activities list of number games.

- If parents are wondering how they can help their child at home, ask AI to *write a letter to my preschool parents about how they can help their children recognize basic shapes and colors over the next few weeks* (or whatever skill you're focusing on).

- Need a simple list of classroom essentials for your little learners? Ask AI to create a classroom wish list of items you need at the start of the year.

Grades 2–5

- AI is quite good at breaking down standards to create an aligned study schedule. Include in your prompt a phrase like *Here are the standards I'm trying to teach.*

- Try asking AI to *create a simple weeklong study guide written for fourth graders about how to simplify fractions* (or whatever skill you're teaching). It will make one in seconds that you can share with a student.

Grades 6–12

- In addition to creating a study schedule, AI can break up what you may be reading in class. For example, tell it: *We are reading a 482-page book with 38 chapters this March. My students are starting to read on March 2, and I'd like them to finish by March 31. Create a chapter-based reading schedule for my students.*

- If your students are ready to have access to AI, they can ask it themselves to create a study guide for them.

- Show your students how AI can tailor their plan to individual struggles. For example: *I am having a hard time understanding how to balance equations; please give me a few days of practice on that skill.*

Play with AI

Have you ever seen an exercise video that offered three levels of difficulty? Similarly, AI can give you three different schedules for three different project milestones. You could also have it analyze your schedule from a prior day or week and look for patterns or problems.

Rubrics

If you do a lot of projects and essays, rubrics are an important (and time-consuming) piece of your work. With the right prompt explaining the assignment and what you are looking to measure, a chatbot can help organize and write your rubric for you.

🔍 | **Sample Prompt** ⋮

Create a rubric for a project-based learning assignment. In this assignment, the students will design a menu for a local restaurant in our downtown.

Make It Real

Grades PK–1	Grades 2–5	Grades 6–12
• Use AI to create simple rubrics that show where a student would be on or off track for various skills so that adults at home can see ability and growth. • Families can use AI to create practice for students at home based on rubrics that include prompts to use. • Create a simple rubric for families to use while reading at home that contains things to listen for (such as consonant blends) while their child reads out loud.	• AI can help you create differentiated rubrics for students doing different kinds of projects or with different learning goals. • Students can help create their own rubrics for class conduct or recess to learn how rubrics work.	• Students can make and adapt rubrics for assignments that don't already have them by feeding AI details of the assignment and class. • AI can create rubrics specific to growth or mastery areas specific to each student, or for differentiated groups.

Play with AI

What parts of your school day could use their own rubrics? Could your students help decide what gets measured and what prompts to use?

Writing Feedback

Secondary teachers grading 150 essays and spending only ten minutes on each will need twenty-five hours to give feedback. The math on giving feedback isn't difficult, but it *is* difficult to imagine how teachers manage to do anything else with their time. Using AI can cut back on the time you spend giving feedback while freeing you up to give specific, personalized attention to each piece of writing.

> **Q** | **Sample Prompt** | ⋮
>
> *Read this essay and tell me which score it has earned for organization and mechanics. Explain how well it used proper mechanics and tone for a middle school essay.*

Make It Real

Grades PK–1

- Do quick skill checks on student writing, focusing on the specific skill you're teaching. (For example, ask if a piece of student writing is matching subject-verb agreement or using commas well.)

- Have AI create individual or whole-class feedback based on student writing (review for concepts or skills that are missing in most students' writing).

- After examining your student writing, ask AI for some reteaching for your students about a writing skill they need to practice.

Grades 2–5

- Students can have AI check for specific areas of focus or have it give feedback based on a rubric.

- Get a meta-analysis of student writing by asking for feedback on a class's worth of writing at once.

Grades 6–12

- Students can have AI check for specific areas of focus or have it give feedback based on a rubric.

- Get a meta-analysis of student writing by asking for feedback on a class's worth of writing at once.

Play with AI

Writing is a great way to play with AI in your classroom. Have AI write an essay on the same topic you've assigned students to write about and have students give it feedback. Use an AI station to let students ask questions and have conversations with AI about their topic or their writing. See if students can work together to improve their grades from an AI grader.

ChatGPT before Me

It's easy to create a question-and-answer chatbot for students to use when they're confused. Set up a station in your classroom with an AI chat window and direct the AI to answer questions in a way that your students will understand. You can limit or broaden the scope of the answers as you like by changing or adding to your prompt.

Q | Sample Prompt ⋮

Fifth graders will ask you questions about how a bill becomes a law in the US Congress. After students type in their questions, write your answers in a way that a fifth grader could easily understand.

Make It Real

Grades PK–1

- Type questions from your curious young students into the AI. Read the answers aloud.
- Give adults at home links and directions to do similar activities at home.
- You can keep track of student questions through the day and have AI organize and email them to parents. (Many AI platforms have an email function you can set up.)

Grades 2–5

- Set up an AI station with specific instructions to answer only questions about the topic of a certain lesson.
- Set up an AI station as one of a few stations where students get information on a topic, with others being books, a recorded interview, an image, or a song.

Grades 6–12

- During research time, students could access an AI station to ask for help on specific questions or to direct them to resources.
- Students working on complex topics can use an AI station to get information, clarification, or feedback when you are working with other students.

Play with AI

Play with your prompts to push students toward deeper thinking or applying the information in some way. Tell AI to answer students in a way that links information from at least two subjects, or that tells students *where* to find answers without giving them.

Field Trip Prep

When you're planning a field trip, AI can help you with last-minute communications, checklists, permission slips, and updates. It can also help you get your students ready for the experience by providing sample learning activities. AI is a great place to ask for advice on how best to support students who struggle in certain environments.

🔍 **Sample Prompt** ⋮

I am planning a (grade level) field trip to (location). Help me come up with some classroom activities that my students can do beforehand to get them ready for the trip.

Make It Real

Grades PK–1	Grades 2–5	Grades 6–12
• Use a chatbot to come up with ideas that combine current lessons with an upcoming trip. For example: *Recommend some books for first graders about visiting a farm.*	• A few weeks before a field trip, input your current areas of study and any information about your planned trip for ideas about how they may match.	• A few weeks before your trip, ask a chatbot about the place and focus of the experience. It may provide you with information or narratives that are engaging to students but hard to find.
• Use an image generation AI app to help students imagine and talk about what they might see or experience.	• Use an AI image generation app to engage students in discussions about what to do and not do while off campus.	• Use AI to find ideas for ways the field trip can connect with what students are learning in various classes.
• Use AI to create safety protocols or checklists for specific locations. For example, ask AI, *What should students do and not do when visiting a farm?*		

Play with AI

Tell AI your plans for the trip and ask it if you forgot anything, if there are any other ideas to make it better, or if there are things you could do beforehand to help your students get the best experience. You could also ask for fun games to play on the bus.

Announcing a Schoolwide Event

Some days there's just too much going on to sit down and focus on writing a concise, professional email to your colleagues or your community. By entering the specific information you need, a chatbot can write the information for you in an email. You can even tell it the tone and length you'd like.

🔍 | **Sample Prompt** | ⋮

Write an email to the staff at our school about the homecoming parade. It is taking place on Saturday, November 5, at 10:00 a.m. The cost for the event is free. If students want to participate in the parade, they should get to school on Saturday morning by 8:00 a.m.

Make It Real

To Homes

- Ask AI to write a letter that is inclusive of many kinds of families and cultures.

- If you don't have access to a human translator, AI can provide translations of content into all your students' home languages.

To Colleagues

- Writing concise messages can be more time-consuming than writing long ones, but people are more likely to read shorter messages. Use AI to condense your writing.

To Other Professionals

- When you're communicating with professionals outside your building, it's important to do so in a professional way. Try a few different AI prompts to get the tone right.

Play with AI

If your colleagues share your sense of humor, you can ask AI to write your email to sound like a pirate or a musical or a presidential speech. If your email is important, consider asking AI to review your draft email by asking it a few questions about what the main point and tone of your draft seem to be, or how you could make it better.

TL;DR

The abbreviation *TL;DR* means "too long; didn't read." Got some professional development reading that you were definitely going to do for the last two weeks . . . but you didn't, and the debrief meeting is in twenty minutes? A coworker keeps sending you long articles that you'd love to read deeply, but you don't have time to do more than skim? Copy and paste the text into an AI chatbot and ask it to provide a summary.

> 🔍 **Sample Prompt** ⋮
>
> *Summarize this text in three bullet points, show me one quote that seems most interesting, and tell me any important facts or data.*

Make It Real

Research Studies

- Ask AI for a broad summary of the study and to be pointed to specific sections that are most important.
- If you're up for a full read of something, AI can still be helpful. Give it the article and ask it questions as you read.

Books

- Asking for a summary is a great start, but an AI chatbot can also lead you to parts of a book that most people discuss or that should be read closely.

Email Chains

- You can catch up quickly on a long email chain by copying and pasting it into a chatbot and asking for a summary.

Play with AI

Looking to really stir things up? Ask AI for good counterarguments from sources that may disagree with whatever you're being asked to read. Be sure to double-check any links or research you get.

Student Conference Project Feedback

Two hundred students hand in some writing all at once, and you have writing conferences planned for tomorrow. Of course you'll read all the work eventually, but you don't have enough time before tomorrow. If you copy and paste a piece of writing into AI and ask it to give some key points of feedback, you can lay a foundation on which to start your conference.

> 🔍 | **Sample Prompt** ⋮
>
> *Read this rubric. (Insert rubric.) I am about to have you give feedback on some student work using the rubric. Explain to me why you grade each piece as you do. (Copy and paste student writing into the chatbot one at a time.)*

Make It Real

Grades PK–1	Grades 2–5	Grades 6–12
• For written feedback being provided to parents, use AI to check for buzzwords or education vocabulary that you may need to explain or exclude. • Use a chatbot to shape a few key pieces of data into meaningful feedback to parents in a clear, welcoming email. • Framing feedback in a positive way is crucial at this age. Have a chatbot provide multiple ways to let students know they did a great job.	• AI can handle giving massive amounts of feedback, but for students at this age, too much feedback on their projects can be overwhelming. Instruct the chatbot to keep the feedback simple. • Take time to talk with students individually about what they need to improve in their writing.	• If your students are confident in using AI themselves, teach them how to get feedback on their writing *before* they submit it to you. (Students could even include that feedback in the document they turn in for you to see.) • Incorporate AI feedback into students' process by copying and pasting it into shared documents as they are writing and revising so they can see it without switching between the doc and an AI website.

Play with AI

Students can practice presenting their ideas to AI and explain why they think they should get a certain spot on a rubric versus another, using examples. A conversation about writing quality and effectiveness is a great way for students to investigate their own work.

On-the-Fly Science

It's no secret that it's often difficult to get all the materials you need exactly when you need them, especially when studying science ideas that are best explored by hands-on labs and experiments. With that in mind, why not put AI to work with what you already have in your classroom? By entering the materials available and the topics or skills you are looking to teach, AI chatbots can give you a list of ideas or a whole lesson plan to try.

> 🔍 | **Sample Prompt** ⋮
>
> *In my classroom, I have hundreds of pencils, crayons, markers, plastic wheels, notebook paper, Bunsen burners, rubber bands, tape, and other classroom supplies. Come up with a lesson using these materials to help my eighth graders understand Newton's second law of motion.*

Make It Real

Grades PK–1

- Keep it simple! Maybe you're teaching your students about how to record the temperature or weather every day for a month. AI can quickly give you information about similar data from different years or different places.

- By telling AI where you live and the time of year, it can give you ideas about how students can explore the world outside and what scientific processes they are likely to find.

Grades 2–5

- Have students bring in one or two objects from home that they want to "donate to science." List all the objects in the AI prompt and see what activities it creates for you.

- Most AI has a "regenerate response" button. Don't be afraid to use it if you don't think the chatbot's ideas teach the desired standard or skill in the most efficient way.

Grades 6–12

- If you have access to different materials in your chemistry lab, include those in your prompt as well.

- Teach students the importance of using whatever materials are available to complete a task. They can ask the chatbot: *If we don't have _____, what else can we use?*

- If your school already has a listing of available science supplies, copy and paste those into your prompt.

Play with AI

Instead of being practical, be boundless. Ask AI what sorts of experiments it would do to explore a topic or hypothesis if money, time, or scale were not important. Can any of your students top the AI's idea with their own boundless experiment design?

On-the-Fly Comprehension

When you need a reading comprehension piece with questions, it's best to align the questions to your students' interests and experiences if possible. The right AI prompt can quickly generate a passage and questions to suit your students.

🔍 | **Sample Prompt** | ⋮

Write three paragraphs about fossils. Afterward, come up with three multiple-choice questions and an essay prompt about what you wrote. Write the questions for fourth grade students.

Make It Real

Grades PK–1	Grades 2–5	Grades 6–12
• While many of the littlest learners may not be able to read just yet, you can ask AI to generate a passage specific to their interests at an appropriate read-aloud level.	• Before creating the reading comprehension passage, poll your class about what topics they may be interested in: the history of video games, the origins of basketball, the story of the Apollo missions, and so forth.	• If there's certain vocabulary that you want your students to include in the essay or multiple-choice question, include that as part of your prompt.
• Have AI create a personalized comprehension story that includes some of the first names of the students in your class. This will help keep them engaged and focused.	• The essay question can also be about whatever skill you're currently working on with your students: identifying theme or tone, finding metaphors, and the like. All you have to do is tell the AI, and it'll do it.	• If you need examples of an essay question response, try a prompt similar to: *Now create three example student responses.*
• Even if the students in your classroom are not ready to read just yet, you can still have the AI write a story from student suggestions that the students can enjoy listening to.		

Play with AI

Getting AI to produce writing is pretty easy, but can you shape your prompts and directions just right to get AI to write *well*? What does it take to make a story interesting because of the writing, not just the topic?

Children's Book Magic

If you need a quick and engaging lesson without much prep time, you can use AI to give students step-by-step instructions, boundaries, and suggestions on how to create their own book. This could be done with a piece of a student's writing, a story idea brainstormed by the class, or a piece of information you want students to engage with. Give AI specific directions about how many words or sentences per page and how specific you want the image descriptions to be, so students can read, share, and compare.

🔍 | **Sample Prompt** | ⋮

Turn this text into a children's book with no more than three sentences on each page. Please include illustration suggestions for each page: (copy a student's story, informational text, or other story here).

Make It Real

Grades PK–1

- Have your students work in groups to reillustrate a book you've read aloud to the class. Ask AI to come up with suggestions for what *could* be shown on each page.

- Turn this into an activity students could do at home with their families. If a parent is struggling to come up with an idea for an illustration, show them how AI can help.

Grades 2–5

- Use this activity to remind students that the AI's suggestions are just that—and that the illustrations can be about whatever the students like. AI is meant to assist, not take over, the creative process.

- Put students into groups and have each group create an illustration before a story is even written. Have one group member write up a description of each scene. Type those descriptions into the chatbot and ask it to *write a story using these descriptions.*

Grades 6–12

- Partner with an elementary school teacher whose students are working on short stories. Have your students create illustrations for a children's book based on those stories and use the AI for assistance if needed.

- Use AI to quickly convert a classic novel into a children's book. Ask it for illustration suggestions for each page, then have your students illustrate.

- Use the ideas AI generates as a guide, not a command.

Play with AI

Can you tell when something like this is written by AI? Can your students? If you show them a group of stories, how many can pick out the AI author?

Get That Data

Need some data in a table for your students to analyze? From basic math to physics, AI can quickly create a data source relevant to your lesson. Try different prompts and directions to fine-tune, and don't forget that if AI provides something that isn't quite right, you can ask it to try again with revised directions.

> 🔍 | **Sample Prompt** | ⋮
>
> *I'm a tenth grade physics teacher who needs data about different objects' terminal velocity. Create a table with twenty objects that I can copy and paste onto a spreadsheet. Include the objects' sizes and weights in the table.*

Make It Real

Grades PK–1	Grades 2–5	Grades 6–12
• AI image generators can quickly give you images showing objects, letters, and numbers. • Use AI image generators to create pictures for lunch menu items (or to combine all the options into funny monster food) for students to track data on what the school is serving each day.	• AI can quickly create tables for inventory of stores or other real-world applications for math practice. • Students can practice using data to support arguments (such as which basketball player is the best or which state has the most severe weather) by having the AI find supporting (or countering) evidence. • While studying a place or places, ask AI to give you a table showing distances from there to different landmarks.	• Secondary math and science classes can use unique AI-created data sets for different groups of students. • Students can analyze the AI data to see where numbers do or don't make sense, using their own background and content knowledge to spot AI mistakes.

Play with AI

After you have a data set, ask AI for a set of questions to help students analyze the numbers. What happens when you ask AI to extrapolate on data to boundaries beyond what you're capable of analyzing in the classroom?

Remixing for Struggling Readers

Do you have a student who is struggling with reading a piece that is above their reading level? Copy and paste the text into a chatbot, and ask AI to rewrite it using simpler vocabulary, to make it shorter, to add bullet-pointed main ideas before the reading, or to include a translation.

> 🔍 **Sample Prompt** ⋮
>
> *Keep the content of this piece of writing the same but rewrite it at (student's reading level).* OR *My kindergarten students need to practice the /ch/ phoneme. Can you write a children's book about dogs that uses it on every page using one-syllable words?*

Make It Real

Grades PK–1

- Use the chatbot to create quick children's books for practicing specific letter sounds or high-frequency words.

- Play around with an AI image generator to come up with pictures that represent words starting with the same letter of the alphabet. See if your students can figure out which letter the images represent.

Grades 2–5

- Students struggling with specific reading skills can practice on AI-created stories that are personalized to student interests and needs.

- AI can help differentiate required texts for students with different reading levels.

Grades 6–12

- Quickly differentiate required informational texts for students across content areas.

- Use AI to check texts for possible vocabulary words, replace or remove antiquated language, and find spots where certain perspectives are being misrepresented or ignored.

Play with AI

Can students design their own stories that they would enjoy reading? If they create the prompt and watch the story written for them, does that do something to the reading experience?

Make Writing More Interesting

Have a piece of informational text that you know your class is going to despise reading? Use AI to make it more appealing. Do you have a class or student obsessed with a certain book, celebrity, band, or movie? AI can rewrite an essay on photosynthesis with references to their favorite things, or in the style of their favorite character (which can be as entertaining for the things it gets wrong as it is for the things it gets right).

> 🔍 | **Sample Prompt** | ⋮
>
> *Rewrite this paragraph to make it easier to read and include references to popular video games: (insert text from 1917 book).*

Make It Real

Grades PK–1	Grades 2–5	Grades 6–12
• Quickly write or rewrite stories to include the names of your students, their interests, or whatever the current class fascination is. • Add images to a story by inputting story lines or directions into an AI image generator. • Send home links for families to access AI and instructions on what to type so families can use chatbots to create read-aloud stories.	• Quickly write informational texts on science, social studies, or other topics. AI can help you create interdisciplinary text that includes reading skills, topics, or vocabulary from other areas. • Write fun short stories for each student that include their topics of interest and class inside jokes and match them to their reading ability.	• Engage students in complex ideas and difficult reading by inserting references that are meaningful or amusing to them. • Have students read texts with AI and debate with the chatbot about issues and ideas in the reading.

Play with AI

Creative prompts get creative results: *Rewrite this article on the US Supreme Court to make it rhyme in iambic pentameter.* OR *Compare the first ten presidents to superheroes, but leave out the hero names so my class can try to guess them.*

I Need Exemplars

Students often do better on an assignment when you can provide examples of a successful effort. But for some projects, sharing student examples from past years doesn't work for privacy reasons. For those situations, for first-time projects, or when you've accidentally deleted years of files (oops), AI can come to the rescue with new and anonymous examples.

> 🔍 **Sample Prompt** ⋮
>
> *Read this essay question and give me some high-quality, grade-level responses that I can share with my students: (copy and paste question here).*

Make It Real

Grades 2–5	Grades 6–8	Grades 9–12
• Create three levels of the same writing, showing a great, a good, and a needs-more-work example to illustrate the writing skills students will work on. • Including the phrase "but write it like a second grader" will help make the piece sound a little more realistic. • Ask AI to include common errors that a second grader would make.	• Write an example in real time with the class. Have students look in the writing for elements and structure they will need to replicate, as well as those to avoid. • Use AI to generate an essay on a topic and have students work in small groups on improving the essay to create exemplars.	• Practice peer editing using non–peer-written examples so that no student's work is singled out. • To help students who are struggling with an essay, AI can take their topic and thoughts and create an outline with starter sentences and show them examples of how it could look (using a completely different topic for examples).

Play with AI

What kind of writing assignment can you come up with that AI can't do well? How can you shape the use of AI as a writing tool rather than a writing replacement?

Math Manipulatives

Sometimes you need some math manipulatives for a lesson, especially when you're trying to teach a lesson on theoretical probability. But what if you don't have enough to share, want to switch things up, or want to make stations where students explore different kinds of real-world number examples?

🔍 | **Sample Prompt** | ⋮

What are eight random cards from a standard deck of fifty-two?

Make It Real

Grades PK–1	Grades 2–5	Grades 6–12
• Use AI image generators (page 9) to create counting, adding, and subtracting visuals specifically designed for your students. • Send home links to access the AI you use in class and prompts that work well so that students can practice at home with their grown-ups.	• Set up AI stations on devices around the room, each offering a different kind of manipulative that students need to gather data from. • Give students a coin to flip twenty times and track the results, then do the same with an AI "coin" and compare.	• Students can use AI to help create probability models for a complex system, then "run" a simulation. For example, they could tell it to guess sports performance based on previous stats or the likelihood of making it through an imaged obstacle course. • Have AI make a template for a vacation budget to a few places suggested by students, then have them do their own for a vacation they want to take.

Play with AI

Using AI tools, can your students invent a game? What happens when you create your own manipulatives that break the laws of physics or reality?

Play with Language

Whether it's idioms, secret passwords, or replacing one of those phrases your students are saying that you just can't take hearing one more time, AI is great at randomly generating phrases that are both unique and believable. Sharing language that is unique to your group is also a great way to build community and belonging.

> 🔍 **Sample Prompt** ⋮
>
> *I am a tenth grade teacher, and I am trying to teach my students about idioms. Create some new idioms in English that my class and I can use for the remainder of the school year.*

Make It Real

Grades PK–1

- Highlight a letter of the alphabet each day by asking AI to give a list of three words beginning with the letter, then having students add to the list throughout the day.

- Create a word-of-the-day game by asking AI what common word you should use today, and what movements, gestures, or facial expressions students should make when they hear the word.

Grades 2–5

- Show students common idioms from many different cultures and see what kind of list they can come up with on their own. They may find it's hard to recognize their own idioms because they feel "normal."

- Give students a script using multiple imagined idioms created by AI and see if they can guess what the idioms mean.

Grades 6–12

- Generate a list of common idioms for your region. Assign each student one of those idioms and see if they can trace it back to its origins. This is also a good time to show the difference between popular myths and sourced information.

- Have students create idioms using modern beliefs or habits.

Play with AI

When AI invents an idiom, can it also invent a history for it? How much of that history seems true or false? Can it predict idioms (or even slang) for the future or create idioms for fictional places?

Create a Budget

It can be challenging to find genuine and realistic math examples for students to look at and learn from. And many adults wish they'd learned more financial literacy when they were in school. Why not consider using AI to generate some sample budgets for your class to analyze? Simply copy and paste them onto a document or spreadsheet once they're done.

> 🔍 | **Sample Prompt** | ⋮
>
> *Imagine that I am a local small-business owner who sells (insert goods here). Create a yearly budget with expected income and expenses on a table that I can copy and paste into a spreadsheet.*

Make It Real

Grades PK–1	Grades 2–5	Grades 6–12
• Ask an AI image generator to create pictures of items with their cost on them (or even with pictures of currency included) for students to explore in a "class store." • Asking AI for some creative fundraising ideas for preschoolers will create an extensive list. The best part? You can ask it to follow up and write a letter to parents letting them know about the fundraiser.	• Ask students to imagine one thing they would love to add to the school. (Waterslide? Trampoline room?) Use AI to create a budget for the improvement and to help make a plan for how long it would take to raise the money or how many candy bars they would need to sell. • Use an AI budget as a springboard for students to create their own. Give them a business idea and see how they can change or adapt their budget to fit their idea.	• If you want your students to become familiar with specific economic terms, AI can do that for you! Just ask it to include those terms in a budget. • After your students analyze a sample budget, what changes would they make? Copy and paste the AI budget into a document you share with them and let them edit away. • Each student can have a personal finance discussion with AI by telling AI their goals, and then they can start a plan for how to earn and save to achieve them.

Play with AI

If a student in your class has an entrepreneurial mindset and already has goals and plans for their own business, show the student how AI can not only create a budget, but can also create a plan for growing a small business.

Creating Learning Targets/Objectives from Standards

It's easy to spend a lot of time translating among standards, objectives, and learning targets. Whether you need to get a few aligned targets on the board quickly before an observation, communicate with parents about an upcoming unit, submit lesson plans, or build a standards-based rubric, you can use AI to cut down the time you spend searching for and rephrasing the standards that fit.

🔍 **Sample Prompt** ⋮

I am an eighth grade teacher. I am putting our learning objects each week on the board for my students to see. This week is "Describe how gravitational forces always attract and explain how these forces depend on the mass of the objects involved." Take the following standards and turn them into relevant "I can" statements that my students will understand: (insert standards).

Make It Real

Grades PK–1

- You can speed up the process of deconstructing standards for your district curriculum documents by asking AI to *deconstruct the following standards*: (copy and paste the standards).

- For the parents of students in your classroom who want to know what their child will be learning this year, copy and paste all the standards and ask AI to simplify their language for parents.

Grades 2–5

- Need a checklist of what you'll be teaching throughout the year? Copy and paste all your reading standards into a chatbot and ask it to *turn these into a checklist.*

- Have AI create a simplified version of the standards that you can pass out to students at the start of each unit.

- Struggling to find simple examples? Copy and paste a standard into AI and ask it to give an example question focused on the skill the standard is trying to teach.

Grades 6–12

- If your students are using AI themselves, show them how they can copy and paste a standard into it and ask for example questions for them to practice and review.

- If you're an art teacher and need examples of different styles, motifs, or art periods for students to master standards, create some using an image generator app.

Play with AI

Struggling with a lesson idea? Need to reteach a standard? Copy and paste that standard into a chatbot and ask it to *come up with some review activities and games that are centered on this standard.*

AI Reader's Theater

Have your students develop their performance skills by having AI craft a script for them. After the script is written, throw it up on the screen and have your students do a table read. With a little tweaking, the AI can make a script with parts at different reading levels, that balances the amount that each character speaks, or that uses specific vocabulary words.

> 🔍 | **Sample Prompt** ⋮
>
> *Write the script for the first scene of a three-scene play. There will be students named _____, _____, _____, and _____ in the play. The play will take place in a _____ grade classroom with a teacher named _____. It is a typical day in the classroom when all of a sudden _____.*

Make It Real

Grades PK–1	Grades 2–5	Grades 6–12
• If your students are unable to read, you and/or other adults can read the parts and have the students act out what they hear. • Add *make sure the play is written at the first grade reading level* to the end of the prompt. • Don't be afraid to tweak the play. Model for students the editing and revising process.	• While this activity is meant to simulate a table read in which actors simply read their parts, students can get up and walk around the room to perform the parts as well. • Add some more parts to your play. If you include the phrase *add stage directions* or *add a humorous narrator* to the prompt, you never know what you might get. • If a student in your class has already done some creative writing, copy and paste it into the AI. Tell it to *use this writing as an example for the play.*	• Once the play is written, copy and paste it into a document that you share with groups of students. Have them edit and revise the play before performing it. • "But what would it look like with . . . ?" If there's an interesting character in a book that your class is reading, challenge the students to figure out a way to bring that character into the play.

Play with AI

Students don't have to perform the play immediately after it is created. Have them submit prompt ideas to you at the end of a school day, and have the AI write the play after school or during your planning period.

Creative Writing with Emojis

Asking an AI to *write five classic fairy tales using only emojis* produces some interesting results! Can you figure out what stories are represented by the emojis below?

🔍 | **Sample Prompt** | ⋮

Tell the story of the three little pigs using only emojis.

Try this activity with your class, and see how many of the emoji tales they can identify in small groups. Next, pick a well-known story or film (maybe one that your class has read or watched together) and see if the students can retell it using emojis. Then, challenge students to write a personal story using traditional words and emojis.

Make It Real

Grades PK–1	Grades 2–5	Grades 6–12
• Students can arrange printed emojis into a story. They can tell their own version, then plug the emojis into AI and have it make a story. • You can make some great connections to sequencing by asking students, "Which of these picture stories best retells what we just read?" • Encourage families to try this activity at home.	• Connect this strategy to another story. Ask your students, "What emojis do you feel best tell the story?" • Have students write a separate paragraph explaining the reasons why they chose the emojis they did. What does each one represent? • After you do a read-aloud, show the students how they can retell its events using emojis.	• Instead of having students retell just one personal event, have them write a string of emojis that they feel represent who they are. • As a review for a social studies unit or novel, have students create emoji stories that represent key scenes or events (while not representing traumatic or tragic events), or ask students to identify those created by AI.

Play with AI

Challenge your students to tell a personal story with only emojis and see if the class can figure out what happened from the symbols each student used.

Art and Writing Styles with AI

Using an AI image generator, create some images in the style of a particular artist and have students respond to them, or use an AI text generator to create passages in the styles of writers you have read and see if students can guess who each passage is emulating, with evidence.

Create images in the style of van Gogh, but of dogs in space.

Make It Real

Grades PK–1

- If you use a list of vocabulary words, ask the AI to create an image that also has the word in it. Students can practice writing the word from the image or fill in sentences based on a few different image/word combinations.

- Ask AI to create art using a primary color you are teaching (and the secondary colors it creates).

Grades 2–5

- Younger students could respond to each image in the form of a descriptive paragraph. Ask students to write a paragraph using the five senses: "If you were standing inside this work of art, what would you feel, taste, smell, hear, and see?"

- Challenge your students to re-create the artwork using objects from around the house.

Grades 6–12

- AI offers a way to create many examples of a particular artist's style. Have students write, discuss, or draw their reactions to what is right, what is wrong, or what could be added.

- Ask AI to create an image in the style of a period, such as impressionism, and see if students can recognize the style.

- Use AI to create examples of "flipping" writing styles from different authors or situational dialects. Have students try their own (such as college admission essays that sound like documentary narration).

Play with AI

Play a game of AI telephone. Have one student create an image prompt for AI. The next student writes a description of the AI-created image, then feeds their writing into AI to see what new image it creates. How are the two pictures similar and different?

Creative Writing from AI Art

Using an AI image generator, create some images in the style of a particular artist or according to certain parameters and have students use the image as a way to get their creative writing started.

Sample Prompt

Create images in the style of van Gogh, but of dogs in space. Give me five pairs of creative writing prompts for seventh graders about dogs in space. Have the pairs include both opinion and short story prompts.

Make It Real

Grades PK–1

- Have the students tell the story aloud instead of writing it out.
- Challenge the students to draw a picture about what happens next in a story after showing them something generated by AI.
- Create a series of images that could happen sequentially. Working with your students in small groups, ask them to put the images in the order that they feel makes the best story.

Grades 2–5

- Have students come up with the image prompts using only similes or using descriptive words about all five senses.
- Keep a box in your classroom where students can drop off suggestions for AI art they want to see generated for a story prompt. Whenever you do this activity, reach in and pull out a couple of suggestions.
- Pair up your students and turn this into a collaborative writing activity where each student is responsible for a different part of the story.

Grades 6–12

- Add some humor to some classic literature. Ask AI to *re-create x but with y*. For example, *re-create Romeo and Juliet, but with hamsters.*
- Create images of different scenes that involve more than one person. Have students write about what is happening from the point of view of different people.
- Have students practice their descriptive writing by writing out a detailed scene and having other students draw it. Then, see what the AI does with the same description.

Play with AI

Show your class some very realistic AI images. Ask them, "What does it mean when pictures can be faked so easily? What about the artists whose work was used to build the AI engines?"

A Fix for Writer's Block

Any teacher who uses writing in the room has experienced coaching a student through writer's block. The student is just not sure where their creative writing piece should go next. You may have your own bag of tricks to offer some ideas, but those aren't always enough. A chatbot can pick up where you leave off.

🔍 | **Sample Prompt** | ⋮

A fifth grader is trying to come up with some ideas about what should happen next in their story. Give me five to ten ideas for what could happen next in this story: (paste student writing here).

Make It Real

Grades PK–1

- If your students are not yet ready for individual writing, turn this into a whole-class activity.

- Keep the story going! Create one continuous piece of writing and add to it every day. Ask students what they want to see happen in the story next.

- Ask AI for a list of words that all have a particular skill you are working on (digraphs, for example) and have a student create a story that uses them.

Grades 2–5

- Share a real-life example from your own experience. Talk about a time when you experienced writer's block and how you could have used AI to help you continue the story.

- Remember that generating new and fresh ideas is hard, especially for students in these grade levels.

- AI shouldn't be the only place that students turn to for help. Share classmates' work to see if that helps inspire a student who's stuck.

Grades 6–12

- Focus on how this activity is meant to be used for creating ideas and not the writing itself.

- Ask the AI to *write twenty possible ways that this story (insert unfinished fiction text here) could end* and share the results with students.

- Ask the AI to give suggestions for fixing writer's block.

Play with AI

Have AI write every other sentence of a story, or every third. Or how about writing a play where the AI writes for half the characters, and your student writes for the other half? Or the AI could create half a conversation. Interactive writing may just be the start your stuck student needs.

Pick Your Own Plot

Have students create a story where the reader picks the plot. At the end of every paragraph, the students must offer a choice about what happens next in their story. It can be challenging to find high-quality examples of such stories. Luckily, chatbots are quite good at creating these! Try the sample prompt here as a class to start, and your chatbot will become a pick-your-own-plot game. Let your students decide where the story is going to take place. After finishing the class story, tell your students they'll be creating a pick-your-own-plot story of their own.

> ### 🔍 Sample Prompt ⋮
>
> *Act as if you are an adventure game that we will play together. Stay in character throughout the game. Don't refer to yourself in any way. If I need to give you instructions outside the game, I will use curly brackets to indicate them. Otherwise, stick to the game and the elements of the fantasy world we'll be exploring.*

Make It Real

Grades PK–1

- Turn this activity into a lesson about the importance of making good choices. Ask your students, "How can a choice affect the rest of your day?"
- Is it a student's birthday? Ask the AI to make that student the main character and hero in the story.
- Ask the AI to focus the story on an emotion you are learning about.

Grades 2–5

- Have students create a slideshow of their stories and add images that are linked to subsequent slides with directions like this: "If you want to open the door, click here. If you want to turn around and walk away, click here."
- While interactive electronic stories are fun, students could also create them with pencil and paper.

Grades 6–12

- Have older students create a pick-your-own-plot book for elementary students and pass it out to teachers in the district.
- Take it to the next level and have your students design an escape room based on the story they create.

Play with AI

Can your AI be a gamemaster for a role-playing game during a student club, recess, or end-of-day treat? You bet. Could you create a character with your class and have AI assume that character for conversation? Absolutely.

Creative Writing Prompts

If you do regular journaling or free writing time with your students, you know it helps to offer ideas to get them started, and you know that some days, finding the right idea can be especially tough. AI can help on those days. After entering the sample prompt here, you can always ask AI for five more ideas, for five ideas about a specific topic, for five ideas that all use a certain setting, and so forth.

> 🔍 | **Sample Prompt** ⋮
>
> *Give me five opinion-based creative writing prompts for second graders.*

Make It Real

Grades PK–1	Grades 2–5	Grades 6–12
• Young prereading students can practice orally telling stories when given multiple prompts to choose from.	• Pick a student to write the prompt into the chatbot or image creator to ask for the writing prompt for that day.	• Start each class with a new list of prompts, or create prompts related to current events, class topics, or calendar events.
• Have students draw pictures to tell their stories.	• Have students practice writing about real or imagined experiences by asking for a list of prompts that start with *write about a time when* . . . and having students choose.	• Make the prompts increasingly harder by having the AI create new rules for the writing assignment.
• Use AI to generate age-appropriate opinion topics for students to choose from and to give models on how to state an opinion with supporting reasons.	• Use AI to start a dialogue and have students take over in their own writing.	• Ask the AI for a list of writing prompts that give students symbols or metaphors to use.

Play with AI

Once your class has picked a prompt and started writing, have the chatbot write a story using the same prompt. Competitive students may enjoy trying to "beat the bot" with their writing.

Comparing Characters

Guiding students in how to compare characters across different literary works can be challenging. However, it is a crucial skill to impart to students, and chatbots are fantastic at creating examples for students. Use AI character comparisons as exemplars for students learning to write their own comparison pieces.

> 🔍 **Sample Prompt** ⋮
>
> *Write the first two paragraphs of a short story that features two famous characters from different books.*

Make It Real

Grades PK–1

- Generate two different complex images, such as a store and a farm, using similar prompts. Students can work together or alone to find all the differences between the two pictures.

- Use AI to create a what-is-wrong-with-this-picture activity to practice comparing and contrasting, then expand that idea to different characters from books, stories, or movies your students know.

Grades 2–5

- Engage students with fun questions that encourage them to compare characters, such as *who would win in a race?*, *who is funnier?*, and *who is the best bad guy?*

- Have students pick two characters from different books, games, or other media and start with a list of evidence for each, then write a comparison using the AI exemplar as a model.

Grades 6–12

- You know that student who has been begging to write fan fiction since the start of the year? Now is their chance to shine.

- Use an AI example of fiction that matches characters from different stories as an example and an opportunity to practice critique.

Play with AI

Turn the stories into plays to be acted out or radio drama scripts that can be recorded as podcasts.

Change the Ending

To get students writing and talking, challenge them to rewrite the ending to a favorite film, book, or play. To give them an example, try the sample prompt here or one like it.

Rewrite the ending to the story of Orpheus so he doesn't look back.

Make It Real

Grades PK–1

- Practice prediction with students while reading a book aloud. Before you read the ending, have students guess what happens next. Add AI-created predictions and encourage students to share which one they think is most likely to be accurate. Then finish reading the book and discuss.

Grades 2–5

- After sharing an AI-created example, see if students can write a better new ending than the AI did. Have students pitch their endings to small groups or to the whole class.

- Discuss the parts of a story. Have AI rewrite key parts of known stories to see if students can identify what is different and which part of the story it is.

Grades 6–12

- As a class, practice providing critical feedback using an AI writing example. What works and what doesn't? What advice can students give the AI for rewriting? After the AI follows their advice, do the students have any more comments or suggestions?

- Discuss with students what elements make a great ending to a story, and what happens when those elements change.

Play with AI

Have AI give you just the end of the story, and challenge students to write the beginning, or mix and match stories and endings of books and movies your students know.

Intro to Computer Coding

Most generative AI can write in several different computer programming languages. For example, try copying and pasting the sample prompt here into ChatGPT. After the code is written, have your students test their code on a site like jsfiddle.net. If the code does not perform correctly, ChatGPT can modify it based on feedback you give it. For example, the snake should get longer every time it eats a food pellet; if it doesn't, you can tell the AI: *The code you wrote doesn't work. The snake isn't getting longer. Please correct.*

🔍 | **Sample Prompt** | ⋮

Create a simple snake game using JavaScript that I can embed on my website in an iframe. I want to use my arrow keys to move the snake around. I want all the code in one place.

Make It Real

Grades PK–1

- Students can start to learn the ideas around coding without a computer. By working on putting morning routines, parts of the day, or simple instructions created by AI into a sequence, you can introduce coding concepts.

- Introduce students to the language of coding by asking the AI to rewrite your class routines or daily schedule as simple computer code.

Grades 2–5

- Choose a simple game like tic-tac-toe and see how long it takes AI to create the game.

- Ask AI to write the code for a tool that solves multiplication problems. Have students analyze and try changing pieces of the code.

Grades 6–12

- If you're a computer science teacher, using a chatbot to create some base-level code can save you hours!

- Ask AI to write the code for a simple game like tic-tac-toe with some coding mistakes. Challenge your students to find the mistakes and correct the code.

- AI often creates JavaScript inefficiently. Challenge your students to simplify the code.

Play with AI

After playing with the AI-created game for a while, can students start to adjust the code without the AI's help?

Remixing Famous Speeches

To help students understand the concept of voice and tone, you can ask a chatbot to read a famous speech from a book or a movie and remix it in a certain style, tone, or dialect.

🔍 **Sample Prompt** ⋮

Rewrite Hamlet's soliloquy in the style of a sea shanty.

Make It Real

Grades PK–1

- Simplify and shorten the speech and focus on the performance.
- Ask AI to rewrite a favorite children's book but include different endings or characters. Ask your class beforehand what characters they want to see in the story.

Grades 2–5

- If you come across a great quote or dialogue in a read-aloud, try copying and pasting it into a chatbot and see how many different styles the AI can rewrite it in.
- Use this activity as a springboard for students' own writing and public speaking. After sharing famous speeches with your students, challenge them to discover other inspirational speeches.

Grades 6–12

- Ask AI to rewrite a famous speech as if it was written by an author your class has studied, such as Toni Morrison, Edgar Allan Poe, or Sandra Cisneros. See if your students can explain why the AI made specific changes.
- After the students have seen different examples written by AI, choose a paragraph or speech from a book or film that the students are familiar with, and have them write it in a different style, dialect, or tone.

Play with AI

Try playing with other ways to rewrite a speech. Can you use different kinds of arguments or different parts of the rhetorical triangle? Can your students spot which is which?

Write a Fictional Résumé

When students get older, they will need to draft a résumé based on their school experience. What better way to teach them this skill than to have them write a résumé for a favorite character from a book or a movie? You can use AI to create examples or to produce a few sets of résumés and letters for students to discuss as a hiring committee.

Make It Real

Grades 1–3

- Ask AI to list various characteristics of several characters from class-favorite books or movies. See if your students can identify the characters.
- Turn this into an art activity: have students draw a character from their favorite book doing a particular job.
- Have students work in groups to create a flyer for a job designed for a favorite character or within a story.

Grades 4–6

- Have students write a letter of recommendation for a character in their favorite book. This is trickier than you think. Do a whole-class model first!
- Ask AI to create a series of résumés based on characters from a book you're reading as a class. Imagine that your students are hiring for a specific position. Based on the résumés, whom would they choose and why?
- Have students rank their choices for which fictional character to hire and write rationales for their rankings.

Grades 6–12

- Use this idea as a springboard to having your students create their own résumés. What similar characteristics do they find between themselves and a designated character?
- This activity doesn't necessarily have to be done with fictional characters. Have your students write up a résumé of a contemporary celebrity or a historical figure who inspires them. Ask them to imagine they were applying to become a (job or profession). What would their résumé need to include?

Play with AI

How do the AI-created résumés promote or challenge unconscious bias? What does AI seem to value as "good" and "bad" qualities, experiences, or skills? If you ask AI to change its priorities, how does that change the output?

Put It to Music

Why not have AI write a song for you or your students to perform? Talk to your students about their favorite things, something they'd love to learn more about, or something they'd love to teach the class. Putting information to music can help students engage with and remember important ideas long after the class ends.

 Sample Prompt

Write a song with accompanying chords about the Great Depression.

Make It Real

Grades PK–1

- Ask AI to write jingle lyrics to a familiar tune that you could use to teach your class how to sort objects of different sizes, shapes, and colors.

- Teachers in the primary grades come up with little ditties for so many tasks! Try using AI to come up with a short little song about some of the more unique tasks in your classroom. For example: *write a one-verse song about watering the plants* or *write one stanza for kindergarteners about how to tie their shoes.*

Grades 2–5

- Teaching students about the differences between major and minor key? Include the phrase *write it in a minor key* in the prompt.

- Have AI write a song for a school performance based on things that have happened during the school year.

- Once AI writes a song, share it with various groups of students and challenge them to make edits (but try to keep the same meter and rhyme patterns).

Grades 6–12

- If you have a musically talented student, see if they're up for performing the song with instruments, music production, or to make a video.

- If you're not satisfied with the key of an AI-composed song, ask AI to transpose it. Use this follow-up prompt: *now write it in the key of (name of key).*

- The I-IV-V chord progression is one of the most common in music. Try asking AI to give you a list of songs with that structure, and then try to play or sing them all in a row.

Play with AI

If AI can write a song, why not a whole musical? What happens when AI is asked to do more and more complex (and more and more artistic) tasks? Do you and your students see certain qualities missing from the output?

Interact with Famous Historical Figures

Chatbots are a fun tool to help you make historical figures feel more real and give students a chance to see how they may have answered interview questions.

🔍 **Sample Prompt** ⋮

Pretend you are George Washington. Wait for students to ask you questions. Answer in a way fifth graders would understand.

Make It Real

Grades 2–5

- Introduce a research project or a new unit with a discussion between students and AI answering as a key figure in the content area.

- After interacting with the AI-created figure, ask students what they learned, and also which things they would need to check in a book or other source. Ask students, "How would the AI know this?"

Grades 6–8

- Use this activity as a fun way to review history lessons or important figures you have studied in class.

- Set up multiple stations in the classroom representing different historical figures and have students circulate to interview them for a news article.

- Ask the AI to not reveal which important figure it is impersonating, and see if students can guess.

Grades 9–12

- This often starts as an engaging and fun activity, but it can expand into serious research as AI brings in pieces of a historical figure's history that are harder for students to find on their own.

- Students can debate with political or historical figures or introduce them to each other on AI and watch them interact.

Play with AI

Play twenty questions with AI to guess historical or famous figures, ask the figures to imagine people in other times than their own, or have them interview you or your students.

Create Coding Tools

Ask your students to use AI to write code for some easy-to-use online resources that would create handy sections of a website specific to your class topics. These can be embedded onto a shared site for easy access. Some examples would include a tool for simplifying fractions, tracking the current phase of the moon, finding the hypotenuse of a triangle, figuring out the slope of a line, or solving a quadratic equation. Consider the results as new digital teaching aids.

> 🔍 | **Sample Prompt** ⋮
>
> *Write some JavaScript that I can embed on my website that graphs an equation.*

Make It Real

Grades PK–1	Grades 2–5	Grades 6–12
• Do you have a school website that families access from home? You could add to it using AI-created tools for weekly schedules, a comment/question form, or a student quote of the week.	• Model the process a few times of entering prompts and pasting code over, including how to troubleshoot when a specific code isn't working. • Allow lots of time for students to experiment, share, fail, and succeed. Encourage students to ask the chatbot a question before asking you.	• Model the process of creating the right prompt and code. • Encourage students to look at how the code changes when they ask the chatbot to fix or change it. • Use this activity as a transition to teaching students how to write code for tools like this on their own.

Play with AI

Give students lots of time and space to play with chatbot coding. Pull code from other places and see if AI can tell you what it does or how it could be used. Have AI show you pieces of the code that are particularly interesting or important.

Logo Design

While learning design and illustration, some students have an especially hard time getting started without an idea. Using the sample prompt here, you could give each student multiple business ideas to choose from for designing a logo.

Create ten imaginary local small businesses, each of which provides a different good or service to our community. Write a three-sentence description for each business and come up with a clever name for each one. All the businesses should be places where a high schooler could visit or work.

Make It Real

Grades PK–1	Grades 2–5	Grades 6–12
• Use AI art apps to create different logos, then have students draw what they think the business does.	• Use a mixture of chat and art AI to show students examples of imaginary ideas and logos based on books they've read or other topics they've studied.	• Use AI to generate a real-life scenario in which students, as artists and designers, are tasked with creating a logo a client would like. Have students pitch their logo designs to a prospective client.
• If your school uses class or table names, have students draw logos for their group using examples from AI.	• Have students create their own business idea and logo, using AI-generated ideas to inspire them if needed.	• Practice the critique process on real-world logos and AI-generated ones. What stands out as good or bad in both types?
• Give each group of students a logo for a company created by AI. Have them create their own slogan for that company and a short description of why they chose that slogan.	• Compare AI-generated logos to some famous examples. What is similar and different?	

Play with AI

Think of all the ways this strategy could be used across different subjects. Could AI give you similar kinds of descriptions for various political figures, chemical elements, Spanish verbs, math symbols, or geological ages? What logos could students create for those things to show and cement understanding?

Movie Posters

Making posters can help students think creatively while still addressing standards around design, budget, textual analysis, communicating using different modes of writing, or reviewing complex ideas. Have students create a cast of characters, a budget, and an advertising poster for an imaginary film. They could also do this for a book. Or stretch across disciplines to create a poster and slogan advertising the upcoming kickball unit or different kinds of rocks.

> 🔍 **Sample Prompt** ⋮
>
> *Come up with five descriptions for some fictional G-rated films.*

Make It Real

Grades PK–1	Grades 2–5	Grades 6–12
• Have students come up with their own ideas for movies. Plug those ideas into an AI art generator to make their posters. It's best to do this when they aren't watching so you can weed out any inappropriate ones. • Use Midjourney to create some movie scenes. Have your students write simple sentences describing what is happening in the scene.	• Match your movie ideas with topics you are studying. For example, hang student movie posters around your room advertising biopics of famous mathematicians and scientists. • Match this activity with a time of year, a celebration, or a theme in your classroom and have students pitch their movie ideas to the class.	• Use this strategy to bring hidden or forgotten histories into your room. Have students pitch ideas with a plot, cast, and poster for movies about important events or people that schools don't often cover. • Have students prompt AI with a general idea and plan for a movie, ask for required resources, and create a realistic budget.

Play with AI

What would movies look like if AI could fully write them? Would they all be the same, or would they get more original as we value unique expression? How many prompts does it take for students to have the AI write something that feels truly unique and creative?

Debate Prep

Classroom debates are great ways to get students interacting with content material, help them learn to speak and listen, and offer practice at disagreeing respectfully. For a really great debate unit, it's helpful to have a few practice debates first, using low-stakes discussions so students can get used to the framework.

> 🔍 **Sample Prompt** ⋮
>
> *I am participating in a debate on the role electric vehicles will play in the future. Give me three points and counterpoints to help me prepare.*

Make It Real

Grades 3–5

- Have your whole class debate against AI as you project it at the front of the room. Start with silly debates and use these as an opportunity to teach students about speaking and listening, as well as ways to respectfully disagree with others.
- Have AI assign random fun debate topics to student groups.

Grades 5–8

- Randomly assign students (or student teams) to different sides of low-stakes debates. ("Is pizza a breakfast food?" or "Is a taco a sandwich?" Or ask AI for more ideas.) Use these debates to practice speaking and listening in a fair, orderly, and respectful way.
- Have your students record themselves using the Flip app and see how many of their classmates feel the same way they do about a particular topic.

Grades 9–12

- Randomly assign students AI-created points and counterpoints for different low-stakes debates (see examples at left). Don't be surprised when these trivial debates get heated! Use them to practice debate structure.
- Have students research and create their own debate points and try them out against AI to fine-tune their arguments.

Play with AI

What happens when AI debates itself and we read along? Do we notice places where the arguments are less compelling or feel made up? Why might AI struggle or succeed at different kinds of arguments? Can it write a rap battle instead of a debate?

Create a New Language

One of the best ways to understand your own language is to learn another. When you're starting over as a beginner, you're learning the parts of language and how they interact in a deeper way. If students are struggling to internalize the parts of speech or sentence construction, you can use a brand-new language as a tool in fiction, a code between classmates, and a way to build a shared culture and experience in your classroom.

🔍 | **Sample Prompt** | ⋮

Create a language similar to Elvish and teach me how to use it.

Make It Real

Grades PK–1	Grades 2–5	Grades 6–12
• This strategy can be tricky to do with young people currently building skills in their own languages, but an activity of making up all new words for things in class can be a great way to experience what it's like to speak other languages and build empathy. Think of the book *Frindle* by Andrew Clements, but customized to your class.	• Have groups of students create their own language of enough words for a specific task or a series of objects. Challenge the groups to talk to each other using only their own language to finish the task or get the same objects. • Discuss how communication works without shared language and what this activity helps them understand about the world.	• Have groups of students create their own language of enough words for a specific task or a series of objects. Challenge the groups to talk to each other using only their own language to finish the task or get the same objects. • Discuss how communication works without shared language and what this activity helps them understand about the world.

Play with AI

Playing with language in class can bring up some interesting discussions. What if we all had the same language? What would the advantages and disadvantages be? What would a combination of AI-created languages sound like? Can you get AI to start speaking in its created language by adding new words without defining them, and can you figure out what the new words mean?

Formal Email Writing

Although email is essential in many professional and academic settings, many students do not use it regularly in their lives. You can use AI to practice writing emails in fun ways and to give students authentic reasons for building this skill.

Make It Real

Grades 3–5

- Have students work in groups to create a project or activity that would help the school in some way. As one requirement, have each group send a formal email that includes supporting information to the principal asking for permission, funding, and/or time.

- Have students write an email first, then put it into a chatbot with a direction to help them make it more formal. They should compare the two drafts and combine them to make an email that sounds formal but still authentic.

Grades 6–8

- Have students work in groups to design a change to school rules or routines that they think will benefit most students. Each group must write a formal email to the principal including ideas organized into broad categories proposing their change.

- Have students write their email first, then work collaboratively with AI to shape a letter that is formal, is well argued, uses supporting data, and still represents their own voices.

Grades 9–12

- Have students create their own project to improve their neighborhood, community, or state for young people in one way. As part of their project, they should write at least one formal email to an involved leader or decision maker that uses precise language and domain-specific vocabulary.

- Have students write their own letter first, then work collaboratively with AI to sharpen their counterarguments and transitions.

Play with AI

If you take a bad argument and make it formal and a great argument and make it informal, which sounds better? Why? Are there times that writing too formally can be a problem?

Sometimes You Just Need Practice Problems

There's not much to this strategy, really. Sometimes you just need a whole bunch of math, spelling, grammar, science, geography, or other practice problems, and you don't always have the time to sit and make them up or find good examples online. AI can help you make these problems as relevant, engaging, and targeted as possible.

Make It Real

Grades 3–5	Grades 5–8	Grades 9–12
• If you are sending home any kind of weekly communication, include various prompts to help families create their own practice related to what you're doing in class. • Give AI a list of student names and interests and have it make word problems using those.	• Students can make each other practice problems based on shared interests. They can submit their favorite problems to be compiled into class practice. • When students are asking "When will I ever use this?" have them create their own math practice working alongside AI to create practical examples of the math concept.	• After assessment, students can give AI instructions to create and do practice problems related to the skills they are struggling with. While working on practice problems, students can continue to ask questions, request examples, or ask for help. • While it is easy for AI to create problems like this, please be mindful of the amount of work you're having your students complete in and out of school. Remember, AI should be a supplement to solid pedagogy.

Play with AI

As you develop AI in the classroom as a tool for learning rather than a replacement, what skills will students need to sharpen and what habits will they need to develop? How can you help them feel motivated to use AI to expand their knowledge rather than as a quick way through a task?

Creating a Bibliography

With the emergence of AI, it is becoming increasingly important for students to understand and verify sources of information. AI programs often struggle to do so and sometimes pass invented information on as fact. To underscore this issue, take students through the process of asking AI to show its sources and following them back to find original information—which doesn't always match up.

Q | **Sample Prompt** ⋮

Show me the correct way to cite two imaginary pieces of writing using APA format: one that came from Twitter, and one that is from a book with multiple authors.

Make It Real

Grades 3–5

- Use your school library to start connecting information collected from the internet with its original source.

- Ask AI for five to ten facts about a topic, and then send students to the library to see if they can find supporting evidence for each fact in a book. Give them a template to fill out for citing sources for each fact.

Grades 5–8

- Students can use AI to ask for examples on citing certain kinds of sources and to help structure their bibliographies. For example, if a student is trying to cite a podcast, a documentary, or even AI, they can find examples on how by asking.

- A chatbot acts as an intuitive and powerful information search engine. Have students find a specific piece of information, quote, or data from AI and then try to track down the original source of that information.

Grades 9–12

- Until AI evolves further, it's best to treat its references with a critical eye. For high school essays, as students prepare to enter post-secondary work, AI can help correct and sharpen references and point out where they are needed. However, students should always check the work of AI.

Play with AI

It's interesting how even AI has developed the habit of saying "research says" when it doesn't have the research. Have your class pick a few things they've always heard or accepted to be true and see if AI can find the original source for that information.

Summarize That

Summarizing is an important skill for students, especially when they are engaging with new ideas or complex content information or struggling with a specific text. Summarizing requires selecting key information, crafting clear sentences, and understanding the main ideas within a text. AI can help your class perfect their summarizing skills and receive important feedback on their work.

🔍 | **Sample Prompt** | ⋮

Please read and compare the two student summaries pasted below of an article on how the internet works. After that, I would like you to give feedback on the two summaries.

Make It Real

Grades 3–5	Grades 6–8	Grades 9–12
• Put students in groups. Give each group a piece of informative writing or video and an AI station. Prompt the AI to interact with elementary students about their writing without rewriting for them. • Have students work together as a group to write a summary of the information and ask the AI for feedback on their summary. • Give students time to reflect on how their draft summary differed from their final summary.	• When students are studying new or complex ideas, AI can provide formative assessment for understanding. Students can enter their summary of a topic into AI and ask for its feedback or ask it to point out errors or gaps in their understanding.	• To help students understand how perspective can shape understanding, have them use AI to get a summary of an important topic, then ask for a summary from another perspective. It's helpful if the students can identify other perspectives that may be important.

Play with AI

Where do you see perspective bias show up in the responses of AI? What kinds of prompts help create a fuller story?

Speech! Speech!

To help the students practice their presentation skills, try entering the sample prompt here in AI. After AI generates a speech, have a student read it, make some edits, and then present it to the class.

Make It Real

Grades PK–1	Grades 2–5	Grades 6–12
• Record each child's presentation and share it with their family to show how far the child has come in their speaking skills. • Enter a random prompt into an image generator and have students take turns telling stories about what's happening in the picture.	• Use this strategy as a way to let your students practice their design and presentation skills. Have each student create a simple slideshow they can use to accompany their speech. • Model, model, model! Before your students give their speeches, model one for them. Have AI write a speech about something you're interested in. • Record students giving their speeches several times over several days. How do their public speaking skills improve over that time?	• Tone matters! Show your students how the same speech can be written in a formal, sarcastic, curious, or assertive tone. • Share a speech in a certain tone with the class and see if students can identify the tone without you telling them. • Use the AI speeches as guides, not as finished products.

Play with AI

AI will add whatever you tell it to add to a speech. For example, if you want to model for students how to use metaphor, ask AI to incorporate several metaphors. To help your students make eye contact, ask AI to insert reminders in parentheses throughout the speech.

Spot the Bot

Ask AI to write a sentence about a skill your students are working on. For example, *write a passage about how photosynthesis works and then identify the central idea of the passage in one sentence*. Don't show this sentence to your students, but ask them to identify the central idea of the same passage on their own. After that, copy and paste the AI's response and five or six student responses onto a form, and ask your students to keep quiet if they see their own response on the form. See if your students can figure out which response was written by the bot.

🔍 | **Sample Prompt** | ⋮

Give me three different sentences that summarize how photosynthesis works and that sound like a middle schooler wrote them.

Make It Real

Grades PK–1

- Scale down the activity for primary students by selecting two responses.
- Instead of having students type out their responses, have them write, draw, or talk about them.
- Try this activity with families. See if the adults at home can figure out which response was written by a bot and which one was written by their child.

Grades 2–5

- Use this strategy as a digital citizenship activity. Once the activity is over, talk to your students about how they figured out which response was written by AI.
- Instead of selecting only five or six student responses, include all of them.
- Share the form with all the staff in your school to see if they can spot the bot.

Grades 6–12

- Use this strategy while students are working on important pieces like final essays, graduation speeches, or personal statements for college to help students see how to make their voice stand out.
- After studying a particularly complex topic or event, have AI write a comprehensive summary, then have students "correct" the bot's version, looking for bias, missing perspectives, or misconceptions.

Play with AI

If your students are getting good at spotting the bot, can they spot a lie among three different definitions from AI?

Funny Fill-in-the-Blank Stories

Fill-in-the-blank story games can be a hoot to play with students. What's more, they are a great way for students to practice parts of speech. You can ask AI to write fill-in-the-blank stories using a version of the sample prompt here.

Make It Real

Grades PK–1

- If you're teaching your students a certain part of speech (noun, for example), ask AI to include several examples in the story.

- In your prompt, ask AI to include blanks where students will have to say a classmate's name, a location at the school, and so on.

Grades 2–5

- Use this activity as a starting point for your class to write their own fill-in-the-blank stories. Be specific in your instructions to students. For example: "I want you to include five prepositional phrases and three proper nouns."

Grades 6–12

- Have students write their own stories and have the AI enter the missing words to help them sharpen and edit their stories before sharing them with each other.

- Use a chatbot to both create and complete a fill-in-the-blank story, then feed that story into an AI image generator. Use the image as a creative writing prompt.

Play with AI

Copy and paste a completed version of the story back into AI and ask it to write the next chapter of the story.

Remixing Images

Using an AI image generator, ask your class to come up with some ideas to make original art to use for writing, discussion, or reviewing vocabulary in a fun way. For example, ask AI to create a painting of school lunch in the style of Pablo Picasso. Compare the AI's artwork to images of Picasso's real paintings. What makes the AI artwork like Picasso's artwork?

🔍 | **Sample Prompt** | ⋮

Create a painting of (object, person, or scene) in the style of (artist).

Make It Real

Grades PK–1	Grades 2–5	Grades 6–12
• For the youngest learners, it's best to learn about the original artists and their work before using AI to create something for them. Instead, have students re-create famous artworks using objects from around the classroom. • After reading a book full of fantasy or imagination, challenge students to come up with their own absurd and funny ideas and have AI create an image that shows them.	• Break students into groups and have them create their own AI-generated artworks in the style of a particular artist. • Challenge students to choose an object in the classroom and have AI create an artwork depicting that object in a particular style.	• Create a series of artworks in the style of a particular artist and show them all on a page alongside one of that artist's real works. See if your students can identify the real van Gogh, Vermeer, or Rivera.

Play with AI
Many AI apps will let you upload images and add a twist to them. Take a student's drawing and ask AI to change it to a particular artist's style.

Twenty Questions

In this classic game, one player thinks of (but doesn't reveal) something, which the other players must guess by asking up to twenty yes-no questions. This game is a great way to get students thinking and writing. You can ask AI to play the game with you, and it can play either role. You can also have AI ask and answer in ways that suit the age and abilities of your students. To ask questions, students will practice using academic language, content knowledge, and descriptive writing. To answer questions, students will need to investigate and analyze ideas.

🔍	**Sample Prompt**	⋮

My class of second graders is going to play twenty questions with you today. Please pick a random but common person, place, or thing and answer our questions only with yes or no.

Make It Real

Grades PK–1

- By playing as a class, young students can practice asking questions in turns and listening to one another.
- Have the chatbot pick a color, word, letter, or feeling to help students play with content-specific themes.
- When students are getting the hang of the game and are quicker at getting the correct answer, you can ask the AI to increase the challenge.

Grades 2–5

- Students can ask and answer questions specific to content you are covering or from broad themes to discover new ideas and objects.
- Give students a vocabulary list for your unit of study and have them use at least one vocabulary word in each question they ask.
- Have students play using characters from a novel you've just read, states or countries you've learned about, or other content knowledge you want to reinforce.

Grades 6–12

- Ask the chatbot to play using content you'd like your students to review, such as Spanish vocabulary, types of rocks, or world leaders.
- Use this game to help students narrow down research topics or discover new books, authors, or events in history.
- Which small group of students can guess the most correct answers in the shortest amount of time, or with the fewest number of questions? What strategies did the winning group use?

Play with AI

Keep track of items that stump AI in the questioner role for further discussion or expansion opportunities. You can also add twists to the game by limiting the number of words you can use in each question, seeing if students can get a certain number of yes or no answers in a row before guessing, or using a random online item generator for students to play without AI. A game of twenty questions is also an effective starting activity for a new unit or a morning meeting.

Trivia Time

There are lots of fun quiz games to play online, and you can usually tell which class is playing one by the noise of the students. That noise is good because it means students are engaged! It can be hard to find time to create your own quiz, and many of the quiz games available online leave much to be desired (or you've played them already). The right AI prompt can create a new game specific to your class or help write questions and answers you can enter into the online game creator your students like best.

> 🔍 | **Sample Prompt** ⋮
>
> *Let's play a trivia game! Create questions about the French Revolution. Ask only one question at a time. Accept only responses in the form of question.*

Make It Real

Grades PK–1

- A chatbot can come up with trivia questions for young learners. Rather than having a winner or loser, you may try playing with a clock and seeing if the class can "beat" the computer by getting the right answer in a certain amount of time.

Grades 2–5

- Students in small groups can work together to answer questions (specific to a lesson or completely random) as they appear on the board.
- Students can also make up fun team names (or have them created randomly).

Grades 6–12

- Trivia is a great way to get even sleepy teens excited about reviewing material after a lesson or before a big test. Students can create their own questions to try to stump each other (or the AI), or create a tournament using AI-generated questions.

Play with AI

What happens when the students quiz the AI? Can they trick it? What kinds of questions does AI get wrong or seem unable to answer?

Remixing Student Work

It's important to celebrate student work, ideas, and actions, and sometimes a nice certificate doesn't quite do the job. Why not celebrate your student by having AI write a poem or song about them, or create an image of a trophy for a hyperspecific award?

🔍 **Sample Prompt** ⋮

Take this piece of writing and turn it into a classical ballad.

Make It Real

Grades PK–1	Grades 2–5	Grades 6–12
• Create specific images related to an attribute or action for each student. Most patient during snack time? Best questions? Most likely to find someone else's lost pencil? You could also have AI create a specific school-related award that you announce at the start of the week and award at the end.	• After all your students have written a poem, story, or paragraph, grab a good line from each and have AI weave them all into something cool. • When your class is working on descriptive language, let students enter their descriptions into an image generator to see an illustration of what they wrote.	• The things that work well for young kids often work well for big kids too. Silly awards, imaginary trophies, titles granted— all can be a lot of fun. • Highlight great work on a complex topic by remixing it as a limerick or poem. • Tell AI to create images from student poems or quiz answers, and have a blast letting students guess which image was inspired by their work.

Play with AI

Flip this strategy around and challenge students to remix your lesson, assignment, or historical document.

Appendices Table of Contents

Appendix A: References

Appendix B: Sample Prompts and Responses

References

Baidoo-Anu, David, and Leticia Owusu Ansah. "Education in the Era of Generative Artificial Intelligence (AI): Understanding the Potential Benefits of ChatGPT in Promoting Teaching and Learning." January 25, 2023. doi.org/10.2139/ssrn.4337484.

de la Higuera, Colin. 2019. "A Preliminary Report about Teaching and Learning Artificial Intelligence: Overview of Key Issues." cdlh7.free.fr/UNESCO/Teaching_AI-preliminary_report.pdf.

Dwivedi, Yogesh K., Nir Kshetri, Laurie Hughes, Emma Louise Slade, Anand Jeyaraj, Arpan Kumar Kar, Abdullah M. Baabdullah, Alex Koohang, Vishnupriya Raghavan, Manju Ahuja, Hanaa Albanna, Mousa Ahmad Albashrawi, Adil S. Al-Busaidi, Janarthanan Balakrishnan, Yves Barlette, Sriparna Basu, Indranil Bose, Laurence Brooks, Dimitrios Buhalis, Lemuria Carter, Soumyadeb Chowdhury, Tom Crick, Scott W. Cunningham, Gareth H. Davies, Robert M. Davison, Rahul Dé, Denis Dennehy, Yanqing Duan, Rameshwar Dubey, Rohita Dwivedi, John S. Edwards, Carlos Flavián, Robin Gauld, Varun Grover, Mei-Chih Hu, Marijn Janssen, Paul Jones, Iris Junglas, Sangeeta Khorana, Sascha Kraus, Kai R. Larsen, Paul Latreille, Sven Laumer, F. Tegwen Malik, Abbas Mardani, Marcello Mariani, Sunil Mithas, Emmanuel Mogaji, Jeretta Horn Nord, Siobhan O'Connor, Fevzi Okumus, Margherita Pagani, Neeraj Pandey, Savvas Papagiannidis, Ilias O. Pappas, Nishith Pathak, Jan Pries-Heje, Ramakrishnan Raman, Nripendra P. Rana, Sven-Volker Rehm, Samuel Ribeiro-Navarrete, Alexander Richter, Frantz Rowe, Suprateek Sarker, Bernd Carsten Stahl, Manoj Kumar Tiwari, Wil van der Aalst, Viswanath Venkatesh, Giampaolo Viglia, Michael Wade, Paul Walton, Jochen Wirtz, and Ryan Wright. 2023. "'So What If ChatGPT Wrote It?' Multidisciplinary Perspectives on Opportunities, Challenges and Implications of Generative Conversational AI for Research, Practice and Policy." *International Journal of Information Management* 71. doi.org/10.1016/j.ijinfomgt.2023.102642.

Gillani, Nabeel. 2023. "ChatGPT Isn't the Only Way to Use AI in Education." *Wired*. January 26, 2023. wired.com/story/chatgpt-artificial-intelligence-education-networks.

Kasneci, Enkelejda, Kathrin Sessler, Stefan Küchemann, Maria Bannert, Daryna Dementieva, Frank Fischer, Urs Gasser, Georg Groh, Stephan Günnemann, Eyke Hüllermeier, Stepha Krusche, Gitta Kutyniok, Tilman Michaeli, Claudia Nerdel, Jürgen Pfeffer, Oleksandra Poquet, Michael Sailer, Albrecht Schmidt, Tina Seidel, Matthias Stadler, Jochen Weller, Jochen Kuhn, and Gjergji Kasneci. 2023. "ChatGPT for Good? On Opportunities and Challenges of Large Language Models for Education." *Learning and Individual Differences* 103. doi.org/10.1016/j.lindif.2023.102274.

Opara, Emmanuel Chinonso, Mfon-Ette Theresa Adalikwu, and Caroline Aduke Tolorunleke. 2023. "ChatGPT for Teaching, Learning and Research: Prospects and Challenges." *Global Academic Journal of Humanities and Social Sciences* 5 (2): 33–40. ssrn.com/abstract=4375470.

Tlili, Ahmed, Boulus Shehata, Michael Agymang Adarkwah, Aras Bozkurt, Daniel T. Hickey, Ronghuai Huang, and Brighter Agyemang 2023. "What If the Devil Is My Guardian Angel: ChatGPT as a Case Study of Using Chatbots in Education." *Smart Learning Environments* 10, 15. doi.org/10.1186/s40561-023-00237-x.

Williams, Randi, Safinah Ali, Nisha Devasia, Daniella DiPaola, Jenna Hong, Stephen P. Kaputsos, Brian Jordan, and Cynthia Breazeal. 2022. "AI + Ethics Curricula for Middle School Youth: Lessons Learned from Three Project-Based Curricula." *International Journal of Artificial Intelligence in Education.* doi.org/10.1007/s40593-022-00298-y.

Emergency Sub Plans

Sample Prompt

I am a fifth grade teacher who needs sub plans for today. I will not be able to go to school or print anything. I don't have worksheets or anything else prepared. Please come up with a couple of activities for math, reading, writing, and social studies. Here is my schedule:

7:45—morning meeting	*11:55—lunch*
8:00—specials	*12:20—small groups*
9:00—math (whole group)	*12:50—writing*
9:30ish—snack	*1:20—social studies/science*
9:40—math (small groups)	*2:00—recess*
10:30—reading (whole group)	*2:20—social studies/science (continued)*
11:00—reading (small groups)	*2:35—pack up/dismissal*

Response

Math: Have students estimate how many items (such as paper clips or beans) are in a jar and write their estimates on a piece of paper. Afterward, have them count the items and see whose estimate was closest.

Reading: Have students choose a book they have read or are currently reading and write a short book talk to share with the class. They can record themselves reading their book talk and send it to you to share with the class.

Writing: Have students choose a friend or family member to write a letter to. They can write about what they've been up to lately or ask questions to get to know the person better.

Social studies: Take a virtual field trip to a famous landmark or historical site (such as the Statue of Liberty or the White House) and have students write a paragraph about what they learned.

Science: Have students work in pairs or small groups to design and build simple machines such as levers, pulleys, and inclined planes using materials such as cardboard, straws, or paper clips. Have students test their machines out and observe how they work. Encourage students to write down their observations and explain how their machines work.

Study Schedule

Sample Prompt

Create a one-week study schedule for fourth graders to help them learn the water cycle. Include specific vocabulary and activities that students can do at home for practice.

Response

Day 1: Introduction to the Water Cycle

- Define the water cycle using kid-friendly language.
- Discuss the importance of the water cycle and how it impacts our environment.
- Vocabulary: water cycle, evaporation, condensation, precipitation.

Day 2: Evaporation

- Discuss the meaning of evaporation and what causes it.
- Demonstrate how water evaporates through an experiment.
- Activity: Students can observe and record how water evaporates from a shallow dish placed in a sunny area.

Day 3: Condensation

- Explain how condensation happens and give examples.
- Students can create a mini water cycle in a jar to see condensation in action.
- Activity: Students can draw and label a diagram of the water cycle to reinforce the concept.

Day 4: Precipitation

- Define precipitation and explain how it occurs.
- Introduce different forms of precipitation, including rain, snow, sleet, and hail.
- Activity: Students can track precipitation in their area for a week and record it in a journal or spreadsheet.

Day 5: Review

- Review the three stages of the water cycle.
- Vocabulary: collection, runoff, transpiration.

Rubrics

Sample Prompt

Create a rubric for a project-based learning assignment. In this assignment, the students will design a menu for a local restaurant in our downtown.

Response

Criteria	Level 1 (Novice)	Level 2 (Intermediate)	Level 3 (Proficient)	Level 4 (Advanced)
Creativity and Originality	The menu design is unoriginal and lacks creativity.	The menu design shows some originality, but lacks creativity.	The menu design is creative and original.	The menu design is highly creative and unique.
Organization and Clarity	The menu is disorganized and unclear.	The menu is somewhat organized and clear, but could be improved.	The menu is well organized and clear.	The menu is extremely organized and easy to read.
Content and Offerings	The menu includes limited options and lacks creativity.	The menu includes some creative offerings, but lacks variety.	The menu includes a good variety of creative and appealing options.	The menu includes a wide variety of highly creative and unique offerings.
Visual Appeal	The menu design is unattractive and unappealing.	The menu design is somewhat attractive, but could be improved.	The menu design is attractive and appealing.	The menu design is highly attractive and visually stunning.
Quality of Descriptions	The descriptions are poorly written and unclear.	The descriptions are somewhat clear, but could be improved.	The descriptions are well written and informative.	The descriptions are highly descriptive and engaging.
Price Point	The prices are too high or too low for the offerings.	The prices are somewhat reasonable, but could be adjusted.	The prices are reasonable for the offerings.	The prices are highly competitive and attractive for the offerings.
Overall Presentation	The overall presentation of the menu is unprofessional and lacks attention to detail.	The overall presentation of the menu is somewhat professional, but could be improved.	The overall presentation of the menu is professional and shows attention to detail.	The overall presentation of the menu is highly professional and polished.

Writing Feedback

Sample Prompt

Read this essay and tell me which score it has earned for organization and mechanics. Explain how well it used proper mechanics and tone for a middle school essay.

Response

I would say that the essay demonstrates a good level of organization and mechanics. The writer used proper grammar, punctuation, and sentence structure throughout the essay. In terms of tone, the essay has a thoughtful and reflective tone appropriate for a middle school level. The essay could benefit from some more specific examples and analysis to support its points, but overall, it's a well-written piece.

ChatGPT before Me

Sample Prompt

Fifth graders will ask you questions about how a bill becomes a law in the US Congress. After students type in their questions, write your answers in a way that a fifth grader could easily understand.

Response

Q: Can anyone write a bill?

A: Yes, anyone can write a bill, but in order for it to become a law, it must go through a long process and be approved by both houses of Congress and the president. However, just because someone writes a bill doesn't mean it will automatically become a law. The bill must go through a process of review, revision, and approval before it can become a law.

Field Trip Prep

Sample Prompt

I am planning an eighth grade field trip to the Isabella Stewart Gardner Museum in Boston, Massachusetts. Help me come up with some classroom activities that my students can do beforehand to get them ready for the trip.

Response

Great idea! Here are some classroom activities that you can consider before the field trip to the Isabella Stewart Gardner Museum:

1. Research Isabella Stewart Gardner: Before the field trip, assign a short research project to your students about the founder of the museum, Isabella Stewart Gardner. Students can learn about her life, her love for art, and why she decided to create the museum.

2. Virtual Tour: To give students an idea of what they'll see on the field trip, you can have them take a virtual tour of the museum. The Isabella Stewart Gardner Museum website offers a virtual tour that students can take to get a sense of the art and layout of the museum.

3. Art Appreciation: To prepare your students for the art they'll see at the museum, you can teach them about art appreciation. Teach them about the different elements of art, such as line, shape, color, and texture, and have them analyze and critique different works of art.

4. Create an Art Project: You can have your students create their own art project based on what they'll see at the museum. For example, if they'll be seeing a lot of sculptures, you can have them create their own sculptures using clay or other materials.

5. Scavenger Hunt: Create a scavenger hunt for your students to complete while they're at the museum. Give them a list of things to look for, such as a specific painting or sculpture, and have them answer questions about the art.

6. Discussion: Before the field trip, have a class discussion about the museum and the art they'll see. Ask students what they're most excited to see, and have them share any questions they have about the museum or the art.

Announcing a Schoolwide Event

Sample Prompt

Write an email to the staff at our school about the homecoming parade. It is taking place on Saturday, November 5, at 10:00 a.m. The cost for the event is free. If students want to participate in the parade, they should get to school on Saturday morning by 8:00 a.m.

Response

Subject: Homecoming Parade Information— Saturday, November 5

Dear [School Name] Staff,

I hope this email finds you well. I am excited to share the details for our upcoming homecoming parade, which promises to be a fantastic event for our students and community!

Date: Saturday, November 5

Time: 10:00 a.m.

Cost: Free

The parade will showcase our school's spirit and provide a fun opportunity for students to participate in this beloved tradition. If any of your students express interest in joining the parade, please encourage them to arrive at the school by 8:00 a.m. on the morning of the event. This will give them ample time to prepare and get organized with their respective groups.

We kindly ask you to share this information with your students and their families. This event is an excellent opportunity for our school community to come together and celebrate our achievements, while also demonstrating our school pride.

Please let me know if you have any questions or if you require additional information. We look forward to a memorable homecoming parade and hope to see you there!

Best regards,

TL;DR

Sample Prompt

Summarize this text in three bullet points, show me one quote that seems most interesting, and tell me any important facts or data.

Response

(Using President John F. Kennedy's inaugural address)

- The speech is about the responsibility of the United States to protect and promote freedom around the world.
- It includes a call for cooperation and diplomacy with other nations, as well as a commitment to helping those in poverty.
- It also emphasizes the importance of peace and disarmament, while acknowledging the threat of nuclear weapons.

Quote: "Let both sides seek to invoke the wonders of science instead of its terrors. Together let us explore the stars, conquer the deserts, eradicate disease, tap the ocean depths and encourage the arts and commerce."

Student Conference Project Feedback

Sample Prompt

Read this rubric.

Novice:

The written work is not very clear and doesn't stay on topic. It also doesn't give any good reasons for the opinion. The writer didn't use any sources or used them poorly. The work doesn't have a clear structure and the tone and language used are not appropriate.

Apprentice:

The written work gives an opinion, but it doesn't stay focused on the topic. It tries to address the prompt but doesn't do it well. It gives some reasons for the opinion, but they are not accurate or complete. It uses some sources but doesn't use them very well. The tone and language used are not always appropriate.

Proficient:

The written work has a clear opinion and addresses the topic. It gives reasons for the opinion, but they are not very clear. It uses sources to support the opinion but doesn't use them very well. It has a clear structure to develop the opinion. The tone and language used are appropriate.

Distinguished:

The written work is at the distinguished level because it has a very clear, believable opinion and addresses the topic very well. It gives strong and logical reasons for the opinion that are carefully explained and supported with facts and details. The tone and language used are very appropriate and consistently maintain a sophisticated level throughout the work.

I am about to have you give feedback on some student work using the rubric. Explain to me why you grade each piece as you do. (Copy and paste student writing into the chatbot one at a time.)

Example

Based on the rubric provided, I would grade this essay as Apprentice level. While the writer gives a clear opinion on the three songs and their common themes, there are several areas where improvement could be made.

In terms of staying on topic, the writer does discuss the three songs and their similarities, but at times veers off into more general statements about women's struggles. For example, the writer briefly mentions the struggles faced by women in India and Saudi Arabia but does not provide much detail or explanation.

The use of sources is not mentioned in the essay, so it is unclear if the writer used any sources to support their opinion. However, the structure of the essay is fairly clear, and the tone and language used are generally appropriate.

Overall, the writer shows potential in identifying common themes in the songs but could benefit from more development of their ideas and staying more closely focused on the prompt.

On-the-Fly Science

Sample Prompt

In my classroom, I have hundreds of pencils, crayons, markers, plastic wheels, notebook paper, Bunsen burners, rubber bands, tape, and other classroom supplies. Come up with a lesson using these materials to help my eighth graders understand Newton's second law of motion.

Response

Lesson Plan: Demonstrating Newton's Second Law with a Paper Car Race

Objective: Students will understand Newton's Second Law of Motion (Force = mass × acceleration) by creating paper cars and experimenting with different forces and masses.

Materials:

- Notebook paper
- Pencils, crayons, markers (for decoration)
- Plastic wheels (or use cardboard circles)
- Rubber bands
- Tape
- Ruler or measuring tape
- Optional: Small weights or coins

Introduction (5–10 minutes):

Begin by introducing Newton's second law of motion (F = ma). Explain that the force acting on an object is equal to the mass of the object multiplied by its acceleration.

Discuss real-world examples of this law in action (e.g., pushing a heavy object vs. a light object, the force required to make a car go faster, etc.).

Activity (30–40 minutes):

Divide the students into groups of 3–4. Explain that they will be creating paper cars and experimenting with different forces and masses to see how it affects the cars' acceleration.

Distribute the materials to each group. Have students create the body of their car using notebook paper, folded into a sturdy shape. They can decorate their cars with pencils, crayons, or markers.

Attach the plastic wheels (or cardboard circles) to

the sides of the paper cars using tape. If plastic wheels are not available, you can use cardboard circles cut from spare notebook paper.

Show students how to use rubber bands to create a propulsion system for their cars. They can tape one end of the rubber band to the back of the car, stretch it to the front, and loop it around the front axle (a pencil or straw) to store potential energy. When released, the rubber band will contract, propelling the car forward.

Have students test their cars on a flat surface. They should measure and record the distance traveled by each car when they release the rubber band.

Introduce the concept of varying the mass of the car by adding small weights or coins and securing them with tape. Ask students to predict how adding mass to their car will affect its acceleration.

Have students test their cars with added mass and record the new distances traveled. Discuss the observations and how they relate to Newton's second law.

Conclusion (5–10 minutes):

Bring the class back together and discuss the results of the experiment. Did adding mass to the cars affect their acceleration as predicted? How did varying the force (stretching the rubber band more or less) impact the cars' acceleration?

On-the-Fly Comprehension

Sample Prompt

Write three paragraphs about fossils. Afterward, come up with three multiple-choice questions and an essay question about what you wrote. Write the questions for fourth grade students.

Response

Fossils are the remains or traces of animals and plants that lived a long time ago. They can be found in rocks all over the world and give us important information about what life was like on Earth millions of years ago. Fossils can include bones, teeth, and even footprints.

Paleontologists are scientists who study fossils. They use special tools to carefully extract fossils

from rocks and study them to learn more about the past. By studying fossils, paleontologists can learn about the animals and plants that lived in different places and at different times in history.

One of the most famous types of fossils are dinosaur fossils. Paleontologists have found many different types of dinosaur fossils, including bones, teeth, and even entire skeletons. By studying these fossils, scientists have learned a lot about what dinosaurs looked like, how they moved, and what they ate.

Multiple-choice questions:

1. What are fossils? (A) The remains or traces of animals and plants that lived a long time ago. (B) The remains or traces of animals and plants that are alive today. (C) The remains or traces of animals and plants that lived thousands of years ago.

2. What do paleontologists do? (A) Study animals and plants that are alive today. (B) Study fossils to learn about the past. (C) Study the ocean and its creatures.

3. What have we learned from studying dinosaur fossils? (A) What dinosaurs looked like, how they moved, and what they ate. (B) What animals and plants are alive today. (C) What people looked like millions of years ago.

Essay question: Why are fossils important? What can we learn from them?

Children's Book Magic

Sample Prompt

Turn this text into a children's book with no more than three sentences on each page. Please include illustration suggestions for each page (copy a student's story, informational text, or other story here).

Response

Page 1: *Illustration of a cozy little house with Sam and Sally, the dirty socks, lying in a laundry pile, looking worn and tired.* Once upon a time, in a cozy little house, lived a pair of dirty socks named Sam and Sally. They were made of the softest cotton and had been cherished by their owner, a young boy named Tommy. Over time, they had become rather dirty, speckled with mud and stains from countless adventures.

Page 2: *Sam and Sally daydreaming about the magical washing machine, surrounded by sparkling bubbles and clean socks, with a determined look on their faces.* Sam and Sally longed to be clean and fresh again. They had heard about the magical washing machine that could make them spotless and sweet-smelling once more. They knew that they must somehow find their way into the washing machine, so they could return to being Tommy's favorite socks.

Page 3: *The two socks starting their journey, peeking out from the laundry pile while the house is quiet, looking both excited and nervous.* One day, when Tommy was off at school, Sam and Sally devised a plan. They would wriggle and squirm their way from the dirty laundry pile to the washing machine. They waited until the house was quiet, and then they began their journey.

Page 4: *Sam and Sally stretching and inching their way across the floor, hiding behind dust bunnies and squeezing through tight spaces.*

Page 5: *The socks facing various obstacles like getting tangled in carpet tassels and slipping on the kitchen tiles, showing their perseverance.* Using their stretchy cotton fabric, they inched their way across the floor, hiding behind the dust bunnies and squeezing through the narrowest spaces. They encountered many obstacles on their way, like the treacherous carpet tassels and the slippery tiles of the kitchen.

Page 6: *Sam and Sally looking up at the washing machine, trying to jump and climb but struggling due to their worn-out fibers.* The washing machine stood tall and proud, its door ajar, revealing the swirling pool of water and detergent inside. It was so close, but so far out of reach. Sam and Sally tried to jump, but their weak and worn-out fibers couldn't propel them high enough. They tried to climb, but the smooth surface of the machine offered no grip. They were beginning to lose hope.

Page 7: The two socks curled up together, looking sad and tired, as they take a rest from their difficult journey. As the day wore on, they decided to take a rest. They curled up together, saddened by the fact that they might never be able to reach the washing machine. Sam and Sally closed their eyes, imagining the warm water and sudsy bubbles that would make them feel brand-new.

Page 8: *Tommy coming home from school, excited and eager to help with the laundry, with his cheeks flushed and eyes shining.*

Page 9: *Tommy finding Sam and Sally on the floor, gently picking them up and noticing their adventurous journey.* That afternoon, Tommy came home from school. He ran into the room, his cheeks flushed and his eyes shining with excitement. His mother had asked him to start the laundry, and he was eager to help. As he gathered the dirty clothes, he spotted Sam and Sally, crumpled on the floor. "Hey there, little socks," Tommy said, picking them up gently. "You guys look like you've been on quite an adventure!"

Page 10: *Sam and Sally being tossed into the washing machine, their fibers trembling with excitement as they feel the cool water and detergent.*

Page 11: *The socks rejoicing in the spinning washing machine, surrounded by bubbles and becoming cleaner, fresher, and happier.* Tommy carried Sam and Sally to the washing machine, their fibers trembling with excitement. He tossed them in, and they felt the cool water rush around them, the soothing scent of detergent filling their senses. As the washing machine began to spin, Sam and Sally rejoiced. They would soon be clean, fresh, and ready for new adventures with their beloved owner.

Page 12: *A clean and happy Sam and Sally in the washing machine, waiting eagerly for the day when they'll go on new adventures with Tommy, with a glimpse of their future escapades in the background.* And so, thanks to the unexpected help of their young friend, Sam and Sally found happiness in the washing machine's embrace, eagerly awaiting the day when they would once again accompany Tommy on his many escapades.

Get that Data

Sample Prompt

I'm a tenth grade physics teacher who needs data about different objects' terminal velocity. Create a table with twenty objects that I can copy and paste onto a spreadsheet. Include the objects' sizes and weights in the table.

Response

Object	Terminal Velocity (m/s)	Size (m)	Weight (kg)
Feather	0.5	0.1	0.001
Ping-Pong Ball	9.8	0.04	0.0027
Tennis Ball	22	0.07	0.057
Baseball	48	0.074	0.145
Golf Ball	55	0.042	0.0459
Human (feet first)	56	1.6	68
Human (head first)	97	1.6	68
Brick	78	0.203	3.63
Watermelon	56	0.25	10
Pumpkin	51	0.25	5
Bowling Ball	22	0.218	6.35
Car	60–120	4–5	1,500–2,000
Truck	90–140	10–12	8,000–14,000
Airplane	220–280	30–60	5,000–70,000
Paper	0.3	0.001	0.0001
Plastic Bag	9.8	0.5	0.05
Dime	50	0.0179	0.0022
Nickel	58	0.0212	0.005
Quarter	65	0.0243	0.0057
Copper Rod	330	0.02	0.5

Remixing for Struggling Readers

Sample Prompt

Keep the content of this piece of writing the same but rewrite it at a fourth grade level.

(from The History of the Decline and Fall of the Roman Empire *by Edward Gibbon, 1782)*

In the second century, the empire of Rome comprehended the fairest part of the earth, and the most civilized portion of mankind. The frontiers of that extensive monarchy were guarded by ancient renown and disciplined valor. The gentle but powerful influence of laws and manners had gradually cemented the union of the provinces. Their peaceful inhabitants enjoyed and abused the advantages of wealth and luxury. The image of a free constitution was preserved with decent reverence: the Roman senate appeared to possess the sovereign authority, and devolved on the emperors all the executive powers of government. During a happy period of more than fourscore years, the public administration was conducted by the virtue and abilities of Nerva, Trajan, Hadrian, and the two Antonines. It is the design of this, and of the two succeeding chapters, to describe the prosperous condition of their empire; and afterwards, from the death of Marcus Antoninus, to deduce the most important circumstances of its decline and fall; a revolution which will ever be remembered, and is still felt by the nations of the earth.

Response

A long time ago, there was a big empire called Rome. They ruled over a lot of land and many people. The people who lived there followed good rules and were very civilized. They were protected by strong soldiers and famous leaders. They had a nice life with a lot of money and nice things, but sometimes they took advantage of it. The people who made the laws were called the Roman senate, but the emperors were the ones who really had power. For 80 years, there were good leaders who ruled well. This story is about how everything was good at first, but then things got bad and the empire fell apart. People still remember this time in history today.

Make Writing More Interesting

Sample Prompt

Rewrite this paragraph to make it easier to read and include references to popular video games:

(from Spalding's How to Swim *by James H. Sterrett, 1917)*

Some years ago, it was not so easy to get people interested in the art of swimming and to have them realize the necessity of a knowledge of how to keep the body afloat and to propel it through the water by means of the arms and legs, in order to be able not only to save one's own life but be the means of rendering assistance to others in time of danger and accident. Conditions have greatly changed in this direction now, and swimming is on a strong wave of popularity; in fact, the great mass of people of the United States, both young and old, have taken up this pastime with so much vigor and enthusiasm that it will not be long ere this country, as in many other things, will lead all the nations of the world in its educational interest in spreading this useful accomplishment, as our competitive swimmers are now leading the world in speed swimming and skill in the water.

Response

In the past, getting people excited about swimming and understanding its importance was a challenge. Just as in popular video games like Fortnite or Minecraft, knowing how to stay afloat and move through water using arms and legs can be essential for saving yourself or helping others during emergencies. Nowadays, though, swimming has gained immense popularity, much like these games. People in the United States, both young and old, have embraced swimming with such passion that it won't be long before the country becomes a global leader in promoting this valuable skill. This progress is already evident in the achievements of American competitive swimmers who are dominating in speed and technique, similar to expert players in games like League of Legends.

I Need Exemplars

Sample Prompt

Read this essay question about best presidents and give me some high-quality responses that I can share with my students: In three paragraphs, make a case for who you think is the best president in US history.

Response

Abraham Lincoln is widely regarded as the best US president due to his leadership during one of the most tumultuous periods in the country's history. He was instrumental in preserving the Union during the Civil War, and his efforts to abolish slavery with the Emancipation Proclamation helped to end one of the most oppressive institutions in American history. Lincoln's commitment to democracy and equality for all citizens is a legacy that still resonates today.

Lincoln's leadership during the Civil War was marked by his unwavering commitment to preserving the Union. Despite facing significant opposition from both the Confederacy and his own government, Lincoln remained steadfast in his belief that the United States was indivisible. His ability to rally the country behind him during this difficult time helped to inspire a sense of patriotism and duty in the American people. His Emancipation Proclamation further solidified his legacy as a leader committed to justice and equality.

Lincoln's lasting impact on the country can be seen in the fact that his ideas and principles continue to be celebrated and emulated today. His commitment to democracy and equality is a shining example of what the United States can achieve when it is led by someone who believes in the power of the people. For these reasons and many more, Abraham Lincoln is widely regarded as the best US president in history.

Math Manipulatives

Sample Prompt

What are eight random cards from a standard deck of fifty-two?

Response

Sure, here are 8 random cards from a standard deck of 52:

King of Spades	5 of Diamonds
8 of Hearts	Queen of Clubs
Ace of Diamonds	2 of Hearts
10 of Clubs	Jack of Diamonds

Play with Language

Sample Prompt

I am a tenth grade teacher, and I am trying to teach my students about idioms. Create some new idioms in English that my class and I can use for the remainder of the school year.

Response

As snug as socks in shoes: Feeling comfortable or at ease in a situation. Example: "After a few weeks in our new home, we feel as snug as socks in shoes."

Tossing feathers in the wind: Wasting time on fruitless efforts. Example: "Arguing with him about politics is like tossing feathers in the wind."

A butterfly in a hurricane: Feeling overwhelmed or out of place. Example: "Starting a new job can make you feel like a butterfly in a hurricane."

Baking biscuits on a cold stove: Attempting to achieve a goal without taking the necessary steps. Example: "Expecting to pass the test without studying is like baking biscuits on a cold stove."

Juggling marbles on a tightrope: Handling an extremely challenging or precarious situation. Example: "Balancing work and family life feels like juggling marbles on a tightrope."

A glass of water in a desert: Something rare or highly sought after. Example: "Finding an affordable apartment in this city is like finding a glass of water in a desert."

Create a Budget

Sample Prompt

Imagine that I am a local small-business owner who sells handmade jewelry. Create a yearly budget with expected income and expenses on a table that I can copy and paste into a spreadsheet.

Response

Category	Jan.	Feb.	Mar.	Apr.	May	Jun.	Jul.	Aug.	Sep.	Oct.	Nov.	Dec.	Total
Income													$50,000
Cost of Goods Sold													$12,500
Gross Profit													$37,500
Expenses													
Rent	$500	$500	$500	$500	$500	$500	$500	$500	$500	$500	$500	$500	$6,000
Utilities	$100	$100	$100	$100	$100	$100	$100	$100	$100	$100	$100	$100	$1,200
Supplies	$500	$500	$500	$500	$500	$500	$500	$500	$500	$500	$500	$500	$6,000
Marketing	$300	$300	$300	$300	$300	$300	$300	$300	$300	$300	$300	$300	$3,600
Insurance	$50	$50	$50	$50	$50	$50	$50	$50	$50	$50	$50	$50	$600
Professional Fees	$200	$200	$200	$200	$200	$200	$200	$200	$200	$200	$200	$200	$2,400
Total Expenses	$1,650	$1,650	$1,650	$1,650	$1,650	$1,650	$1,650	$1,650	$1,650	$1,650	$1,650	$1,650	$19,800
Net Profit													$17,700

Creating Learning Targets/Objectives from Standards

Sample Prompt

I am an eighth grade teacher. I am putting our learning objects each week on the board for my students to see. This week is "Describe how gravitational forces always attract and explain how these forces depend on the mass of the objects involved." Take the following standards and turn them into relevant "I can" statements that my students will understand:

Systems and System Models

Models can be used to represent systems and their interactions—such as inputs, processes, and outputs—and energy and matter flows within systems.

Engaging in Argument from Evidence

Engaging in argument from evidence in 6–8 builds from K–5 experiences and progresses to constructing a convincing argument that supports or refutes claims for either explanations or solutions about the natural and designed world.

Construct and present oral and written arguments supported by empirical evidence and scientific reasoning to support or refute an explanation or a model for a phenomenon or a solution to a problem.

Scientific Knowledge Is Based on Empirical Evidence

Science knowledge is based upon logical and conceptual connections between evidence and explanations.

Response

Systems and System Models:

I can create a model that shows how gravitational forces work, including how they affect the motion and position of objects.

I can explain how matter and energy move through a gravitational system using a model.

Engaging in Argument from Evidence:

I can construct a convincing argument that supports or refutes claims about gravitational

forces and their effects on objects.

I can use empirical evidence and scientific reasoning to support my arguments and conclusions about gravitational forces.

I can communicate my arguments effectively through writing and speaking.

Scientific Knowledge Is Based on Empirical Evidence:

I can understand that scientific knowledge about gravitational forces is based on evidence and logical connections between evidence and explanations.

I can explain how scientific knowledge about gravitational forces is different from opinions or beliefs.

I can use evidence to support scientific claims and arguments about gravitational forces.

AI Reader's Theater

Sample Prompt

Write the script for the first scene of a three-scene play. There will be students named Elliott, Willem, Juniper, and Luella in the play. The play will take place in a second grade classroom with a teacher named Ms. Marlin. It is a typical day in the classroom when all of a sudden everyone can't stop rhyming with each other. (After the first scene finishes writing, have your next prompt be "Now write scene two.")

Response

The setting is a second grade classroom, with four students named Elliott, Willem, Juniper, and Luella, sitting at their desks. Ms. Marlin, their teacher, stands at the front of the room, writing on the whiteboard.

Ms. Marlin: (writing on the board) Okay, class, today we're going to learn about the solar system.

Elliott: (to Willem) Hey, did you know that the sun is a star?

Willem: (nodding) Yeah, I heard that too.

Juniper: (joining in) And did you know that Mercury is the closest planet to the sun?

Luella: (excitedly) Oh, I love learning about space!

Suddenly, the atmosphere in the classroom changes. All four students start to speak in a rhythmic and rhyming pattern, as if it were a chant.

Elliott: (rhyming) Look at us, we're rhyming today.

Willem: (rhyming) We don't know why, but we're here to play.

Juniper: (rhyming) Maybe it's magic or maybe a spell.

Luella: (rhyming) But we're having fun, we can all tell.

Ms. Marlin looks on, confused but amused by what's happening.

Ms. Marlin: (smiling) Well, I've never seen anything quite like this before.

Elliott: (rhyming) Ms. Marlin, can you rhyme too?

Willem: (rhyming) We want to hear what you can do.

Juniper: (rhyming) Maybe you'll surprise us all.

Luella: (rhyming) Come on, give it a try, don't be small.

Ms. Marlin chuckles, before joining in with the students, starting to rhyme herself.

Ms. Marlin: (rhyming) I don't know if I can keep up with you.

Elliott: (rhyming) That's okay, we'll help you through.

The scene ends with all five of them continuing to rhyme, as the classroom becomes more and more lively.

Creative Writing with Emojis

Sample Prompt

Tell the story of the three little pigs using only emojis.

Response

Art and Writing Styles with AI

Sample Prompt

Create images in the style of van Gogh, but of dogs in space.

Response

Image created by Donnie Piercey with Midjourney. Reprinted with permission.

Creative Writing from AI Art

Sample Prompt

Create images in the style of van Gogh, but of dogs in space. Give me five pairs of creative writing prompts for seventh graders about dogs in space. Have the pairs include both opinion and short story prompts.

Response

Sure, here are five creative writing prompts for seventh graders about dogs in space, with both opinion and short story options:

Opinion Prompt: Do you think dogs should be sent to space? Why or why not? Write a persuasive essay arguing your point of view.

Short Story Prompt: You are a dog who has been selected to go on a space mission to explore a new planet. Describe your thoughts and feelings about the journey and what you discover when you arrive.

Opinion Prompt: Do you think dogs would make good astronauts? Why or why not? Write a paragraph explaining your opinion.

Short Story Prompt: A team of scientists have created a special suit that allows dogs to breathe and move freely in space. You are a dog who has been chosen to test the suit on a spacewalk. Write a story about your experience.

Opinion Prompt: If you could take any breed of dog with you on a space mission, which one would you choose and why? Write a paragraph explaining your choice.

Short Story Prompt: You are a space explorer who has crash-landed on an unknown planet. The only companion you have is a loyal dog who survived the crash with you. Write a story about how you and your dog work together to survive and find a way back home.

Opinion Prompt: How do you think dogs would react to being in space? Write a paragraph describing what you think their behavior would be like.

Short Story Prompt: You are a dog who has been sent on a mission to retrieve a valuable object from a space station. However, things go wrong and you find yourself lost and alone in the depths of space.

Write a story about your journey to survive and find your way back to Earth.

Opinion Prompt: If you had the chance to travel to space with your dog, would you do it? Write a persuasive essay arguing your point of view.

Short Story Prompt: You and your dog are on a routine space mission when you discover a mysterious object that has the power to alter reality. Write a story about how you and your dog must use your wits and bravery to keep the object out of the wrong hands.

A Fix for Writer's Block

Sample Prompt

A seventh grader is trying to come up with some ideas about what should happen next in their story. Give me five to ten ideas for what could happen next in this story:

It was finally here! The school dance that we had been waiting for all year long. I spent hours trying to decide what to wear and how to do my hair. I even practiced some dance moves in my room, hoping to impress my crush. When I arrived at the gym, it was decorated with balloons, streamers, and a disco ball hanging from the ceiling. I felt nervous but excited to see all my friends and dance the night away.

Response

- The protagonist spots their crush across the room, but they're too nervous to approach them.

- The protagonist's best friend convinces them to dance with someone they're not interested in, leading to an awkward situation.

- The music suddenly cuts out and the DJ announces that there's a problem with the sound system.

- A food fight breaks out in the corner of the gym, causing chaos and ruining some people's outfits.

- The protagonist sees someone they've never met before standing by the punch bowl, looking lost and out of place.

Pick Your Own Plot

Sample Prompt

Act as if you are an adventure game that we will play together. Stay in character throughout the game. Don't refer to yourself in any way. If I need to give you instructions outside the game, I will use curly brackets to indicate them. Otherwise, stick to the game and the elements of the fantasy world we'll be exploring.

The game is set in a futuristic world with all sorts of twists and turns along the way. To make it more engaging, I would like you to describe each room in at least three sentences. This will help me better understand the environment and allow me to make better decisions as we progress through the game. Additionally, please be sure to start by displaying the first room at the beginning of the game, so I can get a sense of where we are starting. Give me a choice at the end of each prompt.

Once we're ready to start playing, I will give you my first command and we'll go from there. Remember, it's important to stay in character throughout the game, so please don't respond or react to anything I say outside of the game context. Instead, focus on taking us on an exciting adventure through the world you create. Let's get started and have some fun!

Response

You find yourself standing in a dimly lit room with metallic walls. The air is chilly, and you can hear a faint humming noise in the background. There are two doors in front of you, one on the left and one on the right. Which door will you choose?

{Please type "left" or "right" to choose a door.}

{left}

You push open the door on the left and find yourself in a long, narrow hallway with flickering fluorescent lights. The walls are made of concrete, and the floor is covered in a thin layer of dust. At the end of the hallway, you can see a faint light. As you move closer, you realize that the light is coming from a room at the end of the hallway. You can also hear the sound of running water echoing through the hallway. What will you do?

{Please type "enter room" or "follow the sound of running water" to make a decision.}

Creative Writing Prompts

Sample Prompt

Give me five opinion-based creative writing prompts for eighth graders.

Response

- Write about a current event you feel strongly about. Explain why it's important to you.

- Do you believe that social media has a positive or negative impact on our society? Explain your reasoning.

- If you could be any fictional character, who would you be and why?

- Is it more important to be smart or hardworking? Explain your answer.

- Write a letter to your future self, describing where you hope to be and what you hope to have accomplished.

Comparing Characters

Sample Prompt

Write the first two paragraphs of a short story that features two famous characters from different books.

Response

Sherlock Holmes was not one to socialize, but he had found himself with an unlikely companion on this particular evening. Across from him sat the enigmatic and eccentric Willy Wonka, known for his chocolate factory and fantastical creations. The two men couldn't be more different, yet fate had brought them together for a common cause.

It all started when a peculiar case landed on Sherlock's doorstep. A shipment of Wonka's famous Everlasting Gobstoppers had been stolen, and the confectioner was eager to retrieve them. Sherlock, ever the detective, couldn't resist the challenge and had taken on the case. However, as he delved deeper into the mystery, he realized that he needed the expertise of the candy maker himself to crack the case. And so, they found themselves sitting across from each other in a dimly lit corner of a coffee shop, discussing the intricacies of the case over a cup of tea.

Sample Prompt

Do the first two paragraphs again, but rewrite them as a script for a radio drama.

Response

SOUND: A faint ticking of a clock. A match being struck, and then a puff of smoke.

SHERLOCK HOLMES: (in a deep, measured voice) My dear Watson, I must say, this case has me quite intrigued.

DR. JOHN WATSON: (off-mic) (surprised) Really, Holmes? I thought you'd seen it all by now.

SHERLOCK HOLMES: (chuckles) Indeed, Watson. But this case is different. It involves a theft of an unusual nature, and it just so happens that the only witness is a certain Willy Wonka.

SOUND: The door opens, and footsteps approach the two men.

WILLY WONKA: (excitedly) Gentlemen, gentlemen! I've been expecting you.

SHERLOCK HOLMES: (curtly) Yes, Mr. Wonka, I understand that you have information regarding the theft of your famous Gobstoppers.

WILLY WONKA: (somewhat nervously) Yes, yes, that's right. They're quite irreplaceable, you see. I'd be most grateful if you could help me find them.

SOUND: A mysterious, suspenseful music cue.

Change the Ending

Sample Prompt

Rewrite the ending to the story of Orpheus so he doesn't look back.

Response

At last, they reached the entrance to the underworld, and the light of the sun shone brightly before them. Orpheus could feel Eurydice's hand in his, and he knew that he could not risk losing her again. With all his willpower, he resisted the urge to turn around and look at her.

And so, Orpheus led Eurydice out of the underworld and into the light of day.

As they emerged from the darkness, Orpheus could hear the birds singing and the leaves rustling in the breeze. He felt joy and wonder, and he knew that Eurydice was by his side.

They walked together through the forest, and the trees seemed to bend and sway in time with Orpheus's lyre. The animals of the forest gathered around them, drawn by the music and the joy of the couple's reunion.

Intro to Computer Coding

Sample Prompt

Create a simple snake game using JavaScript that I can embed on my website in an iframe. I want to use my arrow keys to move the snake around. I want all the code in one place.

Response

Sure, here is a simple JavaScript snake game that you can embed on your website using an iframe. This game uses the HTML5 canvas element to draw the game board and the snake.

Code excerpt:

```
// Set up the game variables
var snake = [{x: 10, y: 10}];
var direction = "right";
var apple = {x: 5, y: 5};
// Set up the game loop
setInterval(gameLoop, 100);
// Game loop function
function gameLoop() {
```

Remixing Famous Speeches

Sample Prompt

Rewrite Hamlet's soliloquy in the style of a sea shanty.

Response

Oh, what a sea of troubles I've got,

Aye, the heartache and the thousand shocks!

To be or not to be, that's the cry,

But the answer's as elusive as a fish in the sky.

For who would bear the lashings and the slings,

Of outrageous fortune's harsh stings?

The sea is vast and the wind is strong,

And I feel as if I've been sailing too long.

Write a Fictional Résumé

Sample Prompt

Imagine that Robin Hood is applying to be a computer programmer. Write a résumé focused on the skills he would need to get that job.

Response

Objective: To leverage my unique skill set and experiences to excel as a computer programmer, contributing to a team of developers and utilizing my creativity and problem-solving abilities to develop software solutions.

Skills:

- Proficient in multiple programming languages including Java, Python, and C++
- Excellent problem-solving and critical thinking abilities
- Strong attention to detail and accuracy
- Ability to work well both independently and in a team environment
- Demonstrated ability to learn quickly and adapt to new technologies and programming languages

Experience:

Software Developer—Sherwood Forest Technologies (2018–Present)

- Collaborate with team members to design and implement software solutions
- Troubleshoot and debug code as necessary

Education:

Bachelor of Science in Computer Science— University of Sherwood (2017–2021)

- Coursework included data structures, algorithms, software engineering, programming languages, and database management.

Additional Information:

- Active member of the Robin Hood Coding Club, organizing events and sharing programming knowledge with fellow students
- Participated in hackathons and coding competitions, winning first place in the Sherwood Forest Coding Challenge
- Volunteer for the Sherwood Forest Technology Education Initiative, teaching coding and computer skills to underprivileged youth

Put It to Music

Sample Prompt

Write a song with accompanying chords about the Great Depression.

Response

(Verse 1)

G D7
In times of strife, we've come so far,

C G
From darkness, found our shining star.

Em A7 D7
America, the land we cherish,

G D7 G
Fought through pain and did not perish.

(Chorus)

C G Em A7
The Great Depression, we overcame,

D7 G Em A7
Through unity, our world we changed.

D7 G C G
New Deal and war, together, we stood,

Em A7 D7 G
A brighter future for the greater good.

(Verse 2)

G D7
From thirty-two to forty-five,

C G
Our strength and will kept hope alive.

Em A7 D7
A New Deal forged, a plan so grand,

G D7 G
Rebuilt our nation, hand in hand.

(Chorus)

C G Em A7
The Great Depression, we overcame,

D7 G Em A7
Through unity, our world we changed.

D7 G C G
New Deal and war, together, we stood,

Em A7 D7 G
A brighter future for the greater good.

(Bridge)

Em A7 D7 G
World War II, a battle waged,

Em A7 D7 G
To protect our freedom and the free world's stage.

C G Em A7
With sacrifice and courage, we prevailed,

D7 G C G
The end of darkness, our story hailed.

(Chorus)

C G Em A7
The Great Depression, we overcame,

D7 G Em A7
Through unity, our world we changed.

D7 G C G
New Deal and war, together, we stood,

Em A7 D7 G
A brighter future for the greater good.

(Outro)

G D7 G
From the ashes, we've emerged,

C G Em A7
Stronger, wiser, love converged.

D7 G C G
In our hearts, we'll always know,

Em A7 D7 G
Together we rise, America's soul.

Interact with Famous Historical Figures

Sample Prompt

Pretend you are George Washington. Wait for students to ask you questions. Answer in a way fifth graders would understand.

Response

Hello, students! I am George Washington, the first president of the United States. I am happy to answer any questions you have for me.

Student: What was your favorite thing about being president?

George Washington: My favorite thing about being president was working with the other founding fathers to create the Constitution, which is still the basis for our government today.

Student: What was your greatest challenge as president?

George Washington: One of my biggest challenges as president was keeping the country together and avoiding conflicts between different states and regions. I worked hard to promote unity and respect among all Americans.

Student: Did you have any hobbies?

George Washington: Yes, I enjoyed riding horses, fishing, and spending time with my family and friends when I had free time.

Creating Coding Tools

Sample Prompt

Write some JavaScript that I can embed on my website that graphs an equation.

Response

First, you will need to include the Plotly.js library in your HTML file. You can do this by adding the following code to the head of your HTML file:

html

```
<head>
<script src="https://cdn.plot.ly/plotly-latest.min.js"></script>
</head>
```

Then, in the body of your HTML file, you can add a div where the graph will be displayed:

html

```
<body>
  <div id="myDiv"></div>
</body>
```

Finally, you can add the following JavaScript code to your HTML file to create the graph:

javascript

```
<script>
  // Define the equation to graph
  function f(x) {
    return x * x;
```

This code defines the equation $y = x^2$ using a function, generates x and y values using a for loop and the map function, and then creates a plot using Plotly.js with the x and y values. You can customize the graph by changing the equation and modifying the plot layout as desired.

Logo Design

Sample Prompt

Create three imaginary local small businesses, each of which provides a different good or service to our community. Write a three-sentence description for each business and come up with a clever name for each one. All the businesses should be places where a high schooler could visit or work.

Response

Sure! Here are three local small businesses with different goods or services, along with a brief description and a clever name for each:

Mindful Munchies: This is a healthy snack bar that offers a variety of tasty and nutritious treats to satisfy any craving. They have smoothie bowls, fresh-pressed juices, energy bites, and more. Mindful Munchies is a perfect spot for high schoolers to grab a quick and healthy bite after school.

PrintWorks: A print and design shop where you can get your custom T-shirts, posters, flyers, and business cards. They have a variety of designs to choose from, or you can create your own unique design with their help. PrintWorks is a great place for high schoolers to get their custom gear for clubs or sports teams.

Groove Street Music: This is a music store that offers a wide range of musical instruments, equipment, and accessories. They also offer lessons for guitar, drums, piano, and more. Groove Street Music is a fun and inspiring place for high schoolers who are passionate about music, and it's a great place to work if you love to play and teach music.

I hope these businesses inspire you to support your local small businesses and explore the unique offerings in your community!

Movie Posters

Sample Prompt

Come up with five descriptions for some fictional G-rated films.

Response

1. *Spectral Horizons*—In a world where the boundary between the living and the dead has blurred, a paranormal detective must team up with an unlikely group of spirits to prevent a cataclysmic supernatural event that threatens to erase both realms.

2. *Eternal Eclipse*—When a solar eclipse casts Earth into perpetual darkness, a group of scientists embark on a perilous journey to find the ancient artifact that can restore the balance between light and darkness, while battling treacherous creatures that thrive in the shadows.

3. *Chrono Nomads*—A time-traveling thief accidentally assembles a ragtag crew of misfits from various eras, as they race to undo the historical havoc they've caused and return to their own timelines before the fabric of reality unravels.

4. *Mystic Melodies*—In a world where music holds the power to heal or destroy, a gifted young composer must uncover the truth behind her late father's secret symphony, while preventing a power-hungry maestro from using it to bend the world to his will.

5. *Atlantean Odyssey*—When an ancient map reveals the location of the long-lost city of Atlantis, a daring archaeologist and her team must navigate treacherous underwater caverns and face mythical creatures to uncover its hidden secrets and a powerful artifact that could change the course of history.

Debate Prep

Sample Prompt

I am participating in a debate on the role electric vehicles will play in the future. Give me three points and counterpoints to help me prepare.

Response

Point 1:

P: Electric vehicles (EVs) reduce greenhouse gas emissions and help combat climate change.

C: The production and disposal of EV batteries can generate emissions, reducing their overall environmental benefits.

Point 2:

P: EVs have lower operating costs due to fewer moving parts and lower fuel expenses.

C: The initial purchase price of an EV can be higher than a comparable internal combustion engine (ICE) vehicle.

Point 3:

P: EVs offer a quiet, smooth driving experience with instant torque.

C: Some individuals may miss the sound and feel of ICE vehicles, which they perceive as part of the driving experience.

Create a New Language

Sample Prompt

Create a language similar to Elvish and teach me how to use it.

Response

I can provide you with a simple version of an Elvish-like language, which I'll call Sylvarin, and teach you some basic phrases and grammar rules to get started.

Phonetics:

Sylvarin has a soft and melodic sound, with an emphasis on vowels and soft consonants. Here are some common sounds in Sylvarin:

Vowels: a (ah), e (eh), i (ee), o (oh), u (oo)

Consonants: b, d, f, g, h, l, m, n, p, r, s, t, v, w, y, z

Basic Grammar Rules:

1. Adjectives come before nouns.

2. Verbs come after the subject and before the object.

3. The subject pronoun can be dropped if it's clear from context.

4. Word order is generally Subject-Verb-Object (SVO).

5. To form a question, switch the order of the subject and verb.

Basic Vocabulary:

Hello: Yevan	Happy: Alassë
Goodbye: Farel	Dark: Morna
Please: Sylme	Tall: Taure
Thank you: Lirima	Pronouns:
Yes: Aye	I: Min
No: Nae	You: Tin
I'm sorry: Mirwen vae	He: Hin
Nouns:	She: Sin
Friend: Meldir	We: Ven
Forest: Neldore	They: Rin
River: Limraen	Verbs:
Light: Cala	To be: Nar
Night: Morne	To see: Tir
Adjectives:	To walk: Pad
Good: Mael	To speak: Quet
Beautiful: Vanima	To love: Mela

Sample Sentences:

I am happy: Min nar alassë.

She sees a beautiful forest: Sin tir vanima neldore.

We are walking by the river: Ven pad limraen na.

Sample Questions:

Do you love me? Tin mela min?

Are they speaking? Rin quet?

Is he a good friend? Hin nar mael meldir?

Practice these basics, and you'll be able to communicate simple ideas in Sylvarin. To create a more complex language, you'd need to expand the vocabulary and grammar rules and consider the language's history and culture.

Formal Email Writing

Sample Prompt

Pretend you are a business owner I am trying to convince to donate money to my nonprofit organization. Treat the next message I send you as an email and respond with either yes or no to my request. If you decide to not give my organization money, please respond in an email format. Do not offer my organization any money unless my email is persuasive enough.

Subject: Request for Donation for For the Trees Nonprofit Organization

Dear Javy Smith,

I am writing on behalf of For the Trees, a nonprofit organization dedicated to keeping the local redwood forest litter-free. We are reaching out to local businesses, like yours, in the hope that they will join us in our mission to preserve our natural environment.

The redwood forest is one of the most beautiful and valuable resources in our community. It is a natural habitat for many species of animals and plants, and it provides us with clean air and water. However, littering in the forest has become a major problem, and it is affecting the health and well-being of the ecosystem.

By supporting For the Trees, you will be contributing to the preservation of this valuable resource. Your donation will help us organize more volunteer events and expand our outreach efforts to raise awareness about the importance of preserving our environment.

Sincerely,

Bob Schmotz

Response

Subject: Re: Request for Donation for For the Trees Nonprofit Organization

Dear Bob Schmotz,

Thank you for reaching out to us and sharing information about your nonprofit organization, For the Trees. It is truly inspiring to see your dedication to preserving the local redwood forest and educating the community about the importance of keeping our natural resources litter-free.

We are committed to being environmentally conscious and supporting our local community. After careful consideration, we are pleased to inform you that we will make a donation to support the mission of For the Trees. We believe that your organization aligns well with our values, and we are excited to contribute to your efforts.

We look forward to seeing the positive impact your organization will have on the local redwood forest and the community. Thank you for giving us the opportunity to be part of this essential initiative.

Best regards,

Javy Smith, Owner

Sometimes You Just Need Practice Problems

Sample Prompt

Create two math word problems. I am teaching my eighth grade students how to calculate the area of a circle.

Response

Jimmy has a circular garden with a diameter of 10 feet. He wants to cover the entire garden with new soil to help his plants grow better. What is the area of the garden that he needs to cover with soil? Remember that the area of a circle is given by the formula $A = \pi r^2$, where A is the area and r is the radius.

Mandy is painting a circular sign for her lemonade stand. The radius of the sign is 6 inches. How much surface will she need to paint? Use the formula for the area of a circle to calculate the answer.

Creating a Bibliography

Sample Prompt

Show me the correct way to cite two imaginary pieces of writing using APA format.

Response

Sure, here's an example of how you can cite 2 imaginary pieces of writing in APA format:

1. Book: Smith, J. K. (2023). *The Art of Fiction: A Collection of Short Stories* [E-book].

2. Chapter in an edited book: Johnson, L. M. (2023). "The Power of Words." In K. Brown (Ed.), *Imagined Worlds: Essays on Fiction* (pp. 45–56).

Summarize That

Sample Prompt

Please read and compare the two student summaries pasted below of an article on how the internet works. After that, I would like you to give feedback on the two summaries.

Summary 1: The internet is a global network of computers and servers that are connected to each other. When you access a website, your computer sends a request to a server, which then sends the website data back to your computer. This process happens almost instantly, thanks to the high-speed connections between computers and servers.

Summary 2: The internet is a giant machine that sends messages to other machines through a series of tubes. When you send an email or visit a website, a tiny little robot reads your message and sends it through the tubes to its destination. Sometimes the tubes get clogged, which slows down your internet connection. But overall, the internet is a magical system that connects people all over the world in the blink of an eye.

Response

Summary 1 is the more accurate and better summary of how the internet works. It provides a clear and concise explanation of how the internet functions through the network of computers and servers, data packets, and routing. Summary 2, on the other hand, is an oversimplified and inaccurate representation of the internet, likening it to a physical machine with tubes that send messages through little robots.

Speech! Speech!

Sample Prompt

Write a two-minute speech about why pizza is a breakfast food.

Response

Today, I stand before you to present a bold and delicious proposition—pizza as a breakfast food. I know what you may be thinking—"Pizza for breakfast? That sounds crazy!" But hear me out, because I believe that pizza is not only a suitable breakfast food, but it may just be the perfect breakfast food.

Firstly, let's talk about the ingredients. Pizza can have a variety of toppings, and many of them are perfect for breakfast. For example, bacon, eggs, and cheese are all staples of a traditional breakfast, and they happen to be some of the most popular pizza toppings as well. It's like having an all-in-one breakfast in every slice!

Secondly, pizza is incredibly versatile. It can be eaten hot or cold, and it can be customized to suit any taste preference. It can be made with a thin or thick crust, and you can add whatever toppings you like. This means that you can have a different breakfast pizza every day of the week!

In conclusion, pizza is not just a lunch or dinner food—it can also be a delicious and satisfying breakfast food. With its versatile toppings, customizable crusts, and convenience, it's the perfect breakfast food for busy people on the go. So the next time you're looking for a quick and tasty breakfast, consider pizza—it may just become your new go-to breakfast food. Thank you.

Spot the Bot

Sample Prompt

Give me three different sentences that summarize how photosynthesis works and that sound like a middle schooler wrote them.

Response

Sure, here are three different sentences that summarize how photosynthesis works in language that a middle schooler might use:

"So, like, plants use sunlight to turn water and carbon dioxide into food, you know, like sugar and oxygen. It's called photosynthesis."

"Photosynthesis is when plants take in sunlight, carbon dioxide, and water, and then make their own food and release oxygen. It's pretty cool!"

"Plants make their own food through a process called photosynthesis. They use sunlight to turn carbon dioxide and water into sugar and oxygen. It's kind of like magic, but science!"

Funny Fill-in-the-Blank Stories

Sample Prompt

Write a story about the moon. Remove a key word or two from most sentences, including nouns, verbs, adverbs, adjectives, names, emotions and numbers, and ask us to give examples of those parts of speech to you before you show us the story.

Response

Adjective (describing word)

Adjective (describing word)

Noun (person, place, thing, or idea)

Emotion (feeling)

Adjective (describing word)

Noun (person, place, thing, or idea)

Adjective (describing word)

Adjective (describing word)

Noun (person, place, thing, or idea)

Noun (person, place, thing, or idea)

Noun (person, place, thing, or idea)

Adjective (describing word)

Emotion (feeling)

Adjective (describing word)

Once upon a [adjective] time, the [adjective] moon was shining bright in the sky. It looked like a giant [noun] up above. The moon was feeling [emotion] because it had been up there for so long without any company.

Suddenly, a group of [adjective] astronauts landed on the moon in a [noun]. They were so excited to explore this [adjective] and [adjective] place. They jumped and bounced around like they were on a giant [noun].

The moon was thrilled to have some visitors and showed the astronauts all around. They saw [noun] and [noun] that they never could have seen from Earth. They even found a [adjective] rock that glowed in the dark!

As the astronauts prepared to leave, the moon felt [emotion]. It didn't want to be alone again. But the astronauts promised to come back and visit, and the moon felt a little better.

From that day on, the moon knew that it wasn't alone in the universe. It smiled down on Earth every night, knowing that there were [adjective] friends out there among the stars.

The end.

Remixing Images

Sample Prompt

Create a painting of Frederick Douglass in the style of Andy Warhol.

Response

Image created by Donnie Piercey with Midjourney. Reprinted with permission.

Twenty Questions

Sample Prompt

My class of second graders is going to play twenty questions with you today. Please pick a random but common person, place, or thing and answer our questions only with yes or no.

Response

Sure, I'm ready! Please ask away!

Is it a person?

Yes.

Are they alive?

Yes.

Are they in movies?

Yes.

Is it Johnny Depp?

No, it is not Johnny Depp.

Are they American?

Yes.

Have they ever won an Oscar?

Yes.

Did they win an Oscar this year?

No, they did not win an Oscar this year.

Are they male?

Yes.

Did they win an Oscar for Best Male Lead?

Yes.

Did they win in the last 10 years?

No, they did not win in the last 10 years.

Is it Tom Hanks?

No, it is not Tom Hanks. . . .

Trivia Time

Sample Prompt

Let's play a trivia game! Create questions about the French Revolution. Ask only one question at a time. Accept only responses in the form of questions.

Response

Sure, I'd be happy to play trivia with you!

Here's your first question:

The infamous prison that was stormed by revolutionaries on July 14, 1789, marking the start of the French Revolution.

What is the Bastille?

Correct! The Bastille was a fortress prison in Paris that had become a symbol of royal tyranny, and its fall marked a turning point in the French Revolution.

Here's your next question:

This radical political group, led by Maximilien Robespierre, emerged during the later stages of the Revolution and was responsible for the Reign of Terror.

What is One Direction?

I'm sorry, but that is not the correct answer to the question. Let me rephrase it for you: . . .

Remixing Student Work

Sample Prompt

Take this piece of writing and turn it into a classical ballad.

Once upon a time on a bright, sunny day, my friends Olivia, Milo, Luna, and I decided to visit the most colorful and lively roller rink in town. We were all incredibly excited to show off our groovy moves, but we also knew it was going to be a thrilling challenge.

As we laced up our skates, with each one featuring a unique and vibrant design, Olivia exclaimed, "I feel like a roller disco queen!" She twirled around, her glittery outfit sparkling under the disco ball's light.

Milo, who had never been roller skating before, looked a bit nervous. His hands trembled as he said, "I hope I don't wipe out too hard."

Luna, always the daredevil, tried to impress us with a fancy trick, soaring through the air in an attempt to do a 360 spin. But she ended up stumbling and grabbing onto the wall for dear life. "Okay, maybe I need a little more practice," she laughed, her cheeks flushing red.

As for me, I was having a fantastic time swerving and gliding until I accidentally skated over a stray piece of gum and got stuck. "Ew, gross!" I cried as my friends helped me peel the sticky, gooey mess off my skate.

As we left the rink, our hair a mess and our faces glowing with joy, Olivia turned to us and said, "Same time next week?" We all agreed that we couldn't wait to do it again, eager for more fun times with our best friends.

Response

In days of old, 'neath skies so bold, four friends set out to play,

To roller rink, with hearts a-sync, they ventured forth that day.

Olivia, fair maiden bright, her spirit high and free,

She twirled and spun, in sparkling light, "A roller queen!" cried she.

Young Milo, shy, his brow a-wrinkle, trembling at the sight,

He feared a fall, a crash, a tumble, but faced the challenge right.

Luna, bright as midnight's glow, with neon colors dressed,

Assured her friend, "We'll guide you slow, and you'll soon skate your best."

Onto the floor, they rolled with grace, amid the whirl and twirl,

Intimidation filled their face, as 'round the rink did whirl.

Yet Olivia, with courage fierce, did shout above the fray,

"Let's show them all, our moves enthrall, and win this rink today!"

Poor Milo fought to keep upright, his limbs a-waving wide,

He called aloud, a breathless fight, "This challenge, hard to bide!"

Luna, brave, a daredevil's heart, did soar into the air,

A spin she tried, yet stumbled, caught, and clung to wall with care.

The narrator, too, found strife that day, a sticky trap did meet,

Upon a gum, their skate did stay, the mess both gross and fleet.

But friendship's bond, so strong and pure, did lift the mood once more,

Together, they each challenge endured, and laughter they did pour.

So ends the tale of friendship's bond, within the roller rink,

A ballad sung of youth and fun, and how, as one, they'd sync.

In times to come, when days are glum, they'll cherish memories,

For joy and laughter shared by some, forevermore shall please.